Contemporary
African American
Fiction

Contemporary African American Fiction

The Open Journey

Robert Butler

Madison • Teaneck
Fairleigh Dickinson University Press
London: Associated University Presses

Associated University Presses
440 Forsgate Drive
Cranbury, NJ 08512

Associated University Presses
16 Barter Street
London WC1A 2AH, England

Associated University Presses
P.O. Box 338, Port Credit
Mississauga, Ontario
Canada L5G 4L8

The paper used in this publication meets the requirements
of the American National Standard for Permanence of Paper
for Printed Library Materials Z39.48-1984.]

Library of Congress Cataloging-in-Publication Data

Butler, Robert.
  Contemporary African American fiction : the open journey / Robert Butler.
    p.   cm.
  Includes bibliographical references and index.
  ISBN 0-8386-3787-6 (alk. paper)
    1. American fiction—Afro-American authors—History and criticism. 2. American fiction—20th century—History and criticism. 3. Afro-Americans in literature. I. Title.
PS374.N4B78   1998
813'.5409896073—dc21   98-11452
                                                                       CIP

PRINTED IN THE UNITED STATES OF AMERICA

For Mary Jo

It was a very dangerous thing to
let a Negro know navigation
—Olaudah Equiano

Sometimes I feel like a feather in the air,
And I spread my wings and I fly.
—African American Spiritual

For my mother,
who made a way out of no way
—Alice Walker

I revel in fluidity . . . I always
think that we are in process,
making and remaking ourselves
along the way.
—Cornel West

Contents

Contemporary
African American
Fiction

Introduction

A central quest in American life is for pure motion, movement either for its own sake or as a means of freeing oneself from a prior mode of existence. A relatively new and chronically rootless society, America has always set an unusually high premium on mobility. It is not surprising, therefore, that American literature is densely populated with heroes who try "to find in motion what was lost in space,"[1] fundamentally restless people in search of settings which are fluid enough to accommodate their passion for radical forms of freedom and independence. Cooper's West, Melville's ocean, Whitman's open road, and Twain's river are the mythic spaces that our classic heroes yearn for. As John Steinbeck observed of his own travels late in his career, nearly every American has "a burning desire to go, to move, to get under way, any place, away from any Here."[2]

Although American and African American literary traditions differ in many important ways, they are in essential agreement on this way of imagining movement. The journey motif, which is central to both traditions, is often aggressively nonteleological; that is, it usually resists being directed toward a particular place and instead exults in movement through indefinite space. Unlike representative journey books from English and European traditions, American and African American classics are typically open-ended in nature. They characteristically view movement and change as intrinsically valuable—a process of endless becoming rather than progress culminating in a state of completed being. Such open movement becomes a compelling metaphor of the American desire for the "new life," consisting of unlimited personal development.

Whereas, for example, Odysseus travels home to a place in a hierarchical society, Huck Finn heads vaguely west toward a socially open world, attracted, as Ralph Ellison would later be, by the "magical fluidity and freedom" of American life.[3] In the same way, representative slave narratives usually conclude with the central character pointed to the "North"—a state

11

of human liberation rather than a particular place. Tom Jones, Joseph Andrews, and even Robinson Crusoe see their movements as a necessary evil as they look for a stable world that will provide them the definite values they need for a secure identity, but Jack Kerouac longs simply to be on the road itself, intoxicated by its continual novelty and escape from a restrictive society. In a comparable way, the typical blues singer often yearns for open motion as a release from troubles, even though fully aware that the place up ahead is not likely to be very different from previous places. As a result, the blues are saturated with bittersweet images of movement— traveling down an endless highway, leaving town on a fast Greyhound bus, and hopping real freights destined for a mythic North. Robert Johnson pushes such imagery as far as it will go: "You may bury my body, down by the highway side, so, my old evil spirit can catch a Greyhound bus and ride."[4] The blues, which are suffused with what Ellison describes in *Shadow and ·Act* as "a near tragic, near comic lyricism,"[5] are often saved from an enervating nihilism by such surprisingly lyrical images of open movement.

Most studies of modern black fiction, however, argue that it is premised upon narrative patterns that are either flatly static or concerned with various types of failed motion. Blyden Jackson, for example, has contended that

> the world of Negro fiction is as static as the world of the medieval synthesis. It is a world in which the distinctive cosmic process is not change but a holding action. In the typical Negro novel, after all the sound and fury dies, one finds things substantially the same as when all the commotion began. At the end of *Native Son* the world of Bigger Thomas does not differ from that which he has always known. . . . To an overwhelming degree, the universe of Negro fiction is panoramic, not dramatic. It is a still picture. . . .[6]

Roger Rosenblatt, likewise, has argued that representative black fictions envision a "cyclical nightmare" that traps the hero in meaningless repetition leading to "self-disintegration."[7] And Phyllis Rauch Klotman has claimed that movement in modern black literature is useless, since blacks have been denied a "place" in American life and therefore have no meaningful course to pursue.[8] For Klotman, the North, once an equivalent to the West as a symbolic area of possibility for blacks, has been drained of meaning by the disappointments of the Great Migration and other historical betrayals. For this reason, Robert Bone has maintained that black writers from the late nineteenth century to the end of the Harlem Renaissance rejected the picaresque fable in favor of the pastoral, a literary form that celebrates place, a "down home" centering on stabilizing black values and traditions that could offset the traumatic shocks of modern African American history.[9] Lawrence Rodgers defines a very similar position in his recent studies of Great Migration novels written by Paul Laurence Dunbar and Dorothy West. He argues that *The Sport of the Gods* and *The Living is Easy* reject the movement to the North as leading to a falsely materialistic and excessively individualistic lifestyle and embrace instead the South as a culture that presents a "pastoral norm"[10] centered in the traditional values necessary for communal life. For Rodgers, southern place is far more nourishing of authentic black identity than northern space.

But generalizations of this kind must be sharply qualified, because they do not square with a large and significant body of modern black writing that still envisions open movement in a very affirmative way. Although African American literature contains many Bigger Thomases, people who are physically trapped by environments that limit their movement and threaten their humanity, it is also filled with protagonists like Frederick Douglass who are regenerated by sheer movement. And Richard Wright's novels center not only on trapped people such as Fred Daniels and Cross Damon but also on figures like Fishbelly Tucker, who at the end of *The Long Dream* undertakes "a journey that would take him far, far away"[11] toward new possibilities. Moreover, Ellison's hero goes underground not to die but to be reborn via a limitless journey into the self. Once he stops running a race against himself and begins to explore his own inner space, he is well on his way to embracing the "infinite possibilities"[12] celebrated at the end of the novel. Eldridge Cleaver's Stacy Mims, after he is awakened to the true nature of the restrictive society in which he lives, can be liberated by the firm conviction that "life was motion."[13] And many of Toni Morrison's heroines, most notably Pilate from *Song of Solomon* and Jadine Childs from *Tar Baby*, use constant movement through indefinite space as a way of maintaining a vital self in societies that are both racist and sexist.

Houston Baker has argued that because African American literature is centered in what he calls a "blues matrix" it is intensely preoccupied with movement. In *Blues, Ideology, and Afro-American Literature* he claims:

> The guiding presupposition of the chapters that follow is that Afro-American culture is a complex, reflexive enterprise which finds its proper figuration in blues conceived as matrix. A matrix is a womb, a network, a fossil-bearing rock, a rocky trace of a gemstone's removal, a principal in an alloy, a mat or plate for reproducing print or phonograph records. The matrix is a point of ceaseless input and output, a web of intersecting, crisscrossing impulses always in productive transit. Afro-American blues

constitute such a vibrant network. They are what Jacques Derrida might describe as the "always-ready" of Afro-American culture. They are the multiplex, enabling *script* in which Afro-American cultural discourse is inscribed.

Rather than examining African American literature in terms of monolithic ideas or canonical texts that impose a static design upon a literary tradition, Baker sees black literature as a dynamic, ongoing process, "a point of ceaseless input and output" and "a web of intersecting, crisscrossing impulses always in productive transit." His trope for both the blues and African American literature is the railway junction, a space "marked by transience" since "its inhabitants are always travelers." Black literature, therefore, does not rest in a static view of the world nor does it employ "transcendent form" that can freeze experience or stretch it out on a Procrustean bed. Instead, it remains open to the "ceaseless flux" of black life, being careful not to "arrest transience." Because of this, African American literature, like the blues, is "vibrantly polyvalent," a vital dialectic always generating new forms and fresh meanings. For Baker, black literary tradition is always in motion—a "lively scene," a "robust matrix" that is open to "endless antinomies" of human experience, finding in them "conditions of possibility."[14]

Henry Louis Gates Jr. likewise perceives African American literary tradition as a ferment of ideas, an active dialectic in constant motion rather than a static sequence of canonical texts. In *The Signifying Monkey* he argues that black texts form a lively and continuous conversation with each other and works from other traditions; they are always revising each other and thus generating new meanings in an attempt to reflect better the always changing conditions of black life. In such a "self-reflexive tradition"[15] fresh meanings are constantly emerging as a result of a distinctively black rhetorical strategy called "signifyin[g]" in which a given black text repeats and then revises an earlier text. The result is quite different, however, from what Anthony Appiah has called "the Naipaul fallacy"—that is, attempting to valorize a black text by statically echoing motifs from the literature of a dominant society. Whereas the Naipaul fallacy represents what Appiah calls a "post-colonial inferiority complex"[16] because it implies that black writing cannot stand on its own but must be propped up by honorific allusions to canonical works by white writers, Gates describes signifyin(g) in Hegelian terms as a ceaseless dialectic whereby a new black text makes use of previous works by repeating and *revising* them to produce fresh meanings that are distinctively black:

Whereas black writers most certainly revise texts in the western tradition, they often seek to do so "authentically" with a black difference, a
compelling sense of difference based upon the black vernacular.[17]

For Gates, therefore, black literature itself is an open journey, a dynamic
process always producing new texts that comment upon and enlarge the
living tradition of which they are a part.

In many important ways, classic African American fiction in the twentieth century can be seen as artfully signifying upon the open journeys
imagined in nineteenth-century slave narratives. As William Andrews has
persuasively argued, the "black picaro" was a "familiar figure" in pre–Civil
War slave narratives and this important body of literature provided "literary precedents and models"[18] for much subsequent black writing up to the
present day. Frederick Douglass's heroic movement away from the enslaving places of the South to the freer spaces of the North is vividly paralleled
by the invisible man's rejection of the stagnant South in favor of the protean North that offers him "a new world of possibility."[19] Although both
Douglass and Ellison's hero soon find that such open spaces in the North
contain new problems that will continue to vex and entangle them, they
greatly prefer the more open world of the North to the absolutely closed
world of the South. As Ellison observed in *Shadow and Act,*

> In my novel the narrator's development is one through blackness to light.
> . . . He leaves the South and goes North: this, as you see in the reading of
> Negro folktales, is the road to freedom—the movement upward.[20]

Just as Douglass had felt that his "soul was all on fire" because he had
"escaped from a den of hungry lions"[21] in moving from the South to the
North, so too does James Weldon Johnson feel personally transformed when
he enters New York after rejecting his life in segregated Florida:

> The glimpse of life I caught during our last two or three weeks in New
> York . . . showed me a new world, an alluring world, a tempting world of
> greatly lessened restraints, a world of fascinating perils; but, above all, a
> world of tremendous artistic potentialities.[22]

Like William and Ellen Craft, who saw themselves as resembling "Bunyan's
Christian" who had escaped from a "Southern Egypt" to a "city of refuge"[23] in Philadelphia, Langston Hughes, upon entering New York Harbor
in 1925, envisioned the city in quasi-religious terms as a "city of towers

near God, [a] city of hopes and visions."[24] Such a redemptive space, while never simply romanticized by Hughes, was an open process offering a radically new life.

Many twentieth-century black writers, like the authors of many nineteenth-century slave narratives, eventually grew bitterly disillusioned with life in the North, but they only rarely lost their belief in the open journey to free space and usually resumed their quest for such space outside of the United States. Matthew Henson's movement to the virgin land of nineteenth-century Canada, therefore, is brilliantly signified upon by Ishmael Reed's quest in the 1970s for a mythic Canada, a Canada of the mind offering unlimited human and artistic growth. And the Europe in which Harriet Jacobs discovers "freedom" after finding that she was still treated as a "slave"[25] in New York is found in both the lives and works of twentieth-century black writers such as Richard Wright, James Baldwin, and Chester Himes, each of whom left the United States for problematic but much freer lives in Europe.

Several excellent studies concerned with journeys, travel, and migration in African American literature and culture have emerged in recent years, but they are, for the most part, teleological in outlook; that is, they envision such movement as culminating in redemptive fixed places rather than a process of pure motion in open space. Melvin Dixon's *Ride Out the Wilderness: Geography and Identity in Afro-American Literature,* for example, probes the relationship between the achievement of black identity and the experience of "alternate landscapes" such as the wilderness, the underground, and the mountaintop. In Dixon's comprehensive analysis of African American literature from the slave songs to recent fiction by Gayle Jones and Toni Morrison, he argues that "some black writers find resting places . . . of refuge and revitalization" resulting in "a transformation from rootlessness to rootedness for both author and protagonist." For Dixon, the mountaintop is an especially crucial setting in black literary tradition since it provides not only a "height of consciousness" but also a "home" and a "shelter" that stabilizes black identity, rescuing it from the alienation and fragmentation created by mainstream culture.[26]

In a similar way Farah Jasmine Griffin in *Who Set You Flowin'?": The African-American Migration Narrative* carefully explores journeys in representative black texts in terms of how they conclude with black migrants either finding or creating various "safe spaces and other places" in an otherwise hostile world. These havens in place and time may take the form of the domestic "homespace" of the black family, the "sacred space" of the black church, or even the more modest settings of barbershops, "parties, dance halls, and pool halls," which provided travel-weary migrants a sense of community, allowing them to transcend the confusions of ghetto life. For Griffin, black migration from the rural South to the urban North and the more recent "countermigration" back to the South were humanly productive rather than destructive experiences because migrants were able to locate themselves in definite places that were "nurturing, healing, and resisting." She therefore posits a "final vision" of African American migration centered in a "final resting place for black people"—a restored community rooted in reclaimed places.[27]

The focus of this book is quite different, emphasizing the persistently nonteleological nature of the journey depicted in African American literature. Although the exact places to which black *picaros* moved were clearly not unimportant, they usually proved disappointing in the long run. As James Baldwin pointed out in *Nobody Knows My Name*, "Havens are very high-priced . . . the price exacted of the haven-dweller is that he contrives to delude himself into believing that he has found a haven." Like Baldwin, who believed that his "journey had been for nothing"[28] if it needed a final resting point, African American questers keep moving both inwardly and outwardly. Resisting being "placed" in geographical, social, psychological, and spiritual ways, they celebrate a universe that is fundamentally open-ended, that is always becoming new things, and that never rests in a completed state of being.

Cornel West, in describing a recent debate with Afrocentrist Molefi Asante, gave vivid expression to this protean vision of life that is so fundamental to black American literature:

At a very deep level, Molefi Asante and I have clashing intellectual temperaments. . . . For him, notions of a solid and centered identity are positive. I revel in fluidity, in improvisation, in the highly complicated and paradoxical. Asante and I agree in our critiques of white supremacy; we agree in speaking to issues of self-love and self-respect among people of African descent. We end there. He advocates a conception of self that is grounded in a unified field of African culture. But that way of framing the question is alien to me. I'm not for a solid anything. I begin with a radical cultural hybridity, an improvisational New World sensibility. I always think that we are in process, making and remaking ourselves along the way. I see it in Louis Armstrong, I see it in Sarah Vaughn, I see it in Emerson's essays, I see it in Whitman's poetry about democratic vistas.[29]

Seeing himself as part of a hybrid culture that is a dynamic mixture of constantly changing elements, West refuses to be "grounded" in any one culture or any set of rigid absolutes and attributes to himself an "improvisational New World sensibility" that "revel[s] in fluidity." Like Ellison who affirmed the "magical fluidity of American life,"[30] he is suspicious of the "solid and centered identity" extolled by Asante because he fears it will do violence to the complexity and richness of both his own personality and African American culture. Indeed, he is "not for a solid anything," preferring instead to be an always-evolving self engaged in the sort of endless journey described by Emerson and Whitman and exemplified in the lives of black artists such as Sarah Vaughn and Louis Armstrong.

Paul Gilroy, in his provocative study *The Black Atlantic*, shares West's concerns about absolutist theories that reduce black experience to a fixed state of being. Rejecting all essentialist visions of history and human identity, he conceives of the experience of "black Atlantic" people in America, England, and the Caribbean as an ongoing journey in which "movement, relocation, and restlessness are the norms rather than exceptions." Gilroy describes the black Atlantic diaspora as "a tradition in ceaseless motion" that is much better known for its "routes" than its "roots." Like West, he celebrates this prospect in both its personal and cultural manifestations, emphasizing that such a dynamic view of the self, culture, and history affirms a world that is always creatively evolving: "The history of the black Atlantic yields a course of lessons to the instability and mutability of identities which are always unfinished, always being remade."[31]

The nine novels examined in this study explore in a rich variety of ways how the "mutability" of African American life gives rise to a potent "New World sensibility" that exults in constant movement leading to limitless growth. Each of these nine major texts dramatizes open journeys to various types and varying degrees of freedom and self-creation. The first chapter focuses upon Richard Wright's *Native Son* and Zora Neale Hurston's *Their Eyes Were Watching God*, two seminal texts that go to the heart of the American racial dilemma by exploring the conflict between their central characters' profound desires for open motion and their culture's imperative that they remain within their "place." Whereas Bigger Thomas's deepest promptings urge him to "fly" beyond the harsh determinants of his social world, his society surrounds him with literal and symbolic walls that reduce him to the level of a slave. The novel's naturalistic outer narrative depicts Bigger's gradual decline into the status of a victim confined in a jail cell awaiting a death sentence. But the novel's inner, existential narrative tells a very different story, dramatizing his open journey to the self, following "a strange path in a strange land" down "some road to a sure and quiet knowledge."[32] The meaning of *Native Son* lies in the dialectical tension of these two opposed narratives. In a similar way, *Their Eyes Were Watching God* is centered in a polarity between stasis and open movement. While Janie Crawford's social environment attempts to fix her in a place which imposes a rigidly stereotypical identity upon her, her imagination and spirit yearn for open space, a "horizon," which offers a protean self.

While *Native Son* and *Their Eyes Were Watching God* can only provide the faint outlines of such an open journey to self because their narratives conclude with central characters imagining but not fully achieving an open journey into their own inner space and into the external space of the worlds in which they live, Ellison's *Invisible Man* takes up precisely where Wright's and Hurston's novels leave off, giving full and convincing novelistic form to the open journey. Using a variety of surrealistic techniques, Ellison transfigures the physical setting in which the hero lives, turning a restrictive place into a series of liberating spaces. The urban landscape, outwardly resembling the sort of ghetto that traps Bigger Thomas, becomes a mindscape, a psychological world offering new possibilities. The underground room in which the hero takes up residence is transformed from a tomb into a womb, a source of power and new life, becoming a modern equivalent to two liberating spaces from classic American literature of the nineteenth century. Even though it has been "shut off and forgotten in the nineteenth century," it can be opened by the hero's act of will and imagination, thus making it a "dimensionless room" with "space, unbroken,"[33] a psychological frontier offering the hero the inner space he needs to achieve a new life. It is also symbolically linked with the Underground Railroad, another free space offering the hero new possibilities for growth. Ellison's novel thus celebrates the magical fluidity and freedom of American life, envisioning America as a problematic but open world inviting the hero to assume a protean identity as a black Odysseus, a modern-day Frederick Douglass.

The third chapter focuses on Alice Walker's *The Third Life of Grange Copeland*. It examines how this novel reverses a major trend in American fiction by centering on a female character who is a genuine picaresque figure capable of liberating herself by living her life as an open journey. American fiction about women is, for the most part, a literature of enclosure in which the heroine either accommodates herself to marriage and the securities of place or rebels against the settled life but can find no viable alternative to it. Hawthorne's Hester Prynne, for example, asks Dimmesdale to leave Boston with her so that the two might move toward a new life, but he lacks the nerve to do so and she is finally condemned to remain in the place where they have sinned and atones for their mistakes by assuming the traditional women's role of nurse. James's Isabel Archer, who refuses to divorce her husband even after she has discovered his infidelities, stays in Italy and tries to fulfill herself in the role of mother. More rebellious figures such as Chopin's Edna Pontillier and Wharton's Lily Bart reject the places assigned to them by a patriarchal society but can create no new spaces for themselves in American life and eventually commit suicide. Even more recent works, such as Nella Larsen's *Quicksand*, Anne Petry's *The Street*, Sylvia Plath's *The Bell Jar*, and Judith Rossner's *Looking for Mr. Goodbar*, portray their female protagonists as hopelessly trapped. But Walker's *The Third Life of Grange Copeland* is a dramatic reversal of these patterns of entrapment, since by living her life as an open journey, its heroine Ruth Copeland is able to achieve the radical forms of freedom and independence that American male picaros claim for themselves. Rejecting marriage and the securities of place, she defines her life as continuous movement (in both political and personal terms), thus earning a kind of heroic status that women in American fiction rarely achieve.

The fourth chapter centers on Toni Morrison's *Song of Solomon*, a novel that offers another complex variation on the journey motif in black literature. It is careful not to endorse uncritically either open motion or its opposite, placement in a stable society. Instead, the novel grows out of an intricate dialectic between the possibilities of space and place, which are seen as options that may be used well or poorly. Open motion, what Morrison often describes as "soaring" and "flying," can destroy as well as liberate. In the same way, attachment to a community rooted in tradition and place can either be a trap or a stabilizing force. The novel therefore presents a tough-minded interplay of opposite ideas that never come to rest in any simple resolution. Refusing to celebrate naively the myth of open motion as does Kerouac's *On the Road*, it nevertheless does not categorically reject the myth as does Barth's *The End of the Road*. Morrison's themes are themselves in constant motion, a dialectical ferment of ideas that generate new ideas with each reading.

The fifth chapter examines Charles Johnson's *Faith and the Good Thing*, a novel that provides another perspective on the open journey in Afro-American literature. For Johnson this journey is perceived in metaphysical terms as an endless quest for truths that are always evolving into new forms. His heroine's task, therefore, is to break away from all static, fixed conceptions of reality and to apprehend life in fluid terms as ceaseless change, continuous growth. As Faith discovers from her mentor, the Swamp Lady, "There ain't no beginnin' and there ain't no end. There's only searchin' and sufferin'."[34] Understanding this, she breaks away from her earlier teleological conception of life as a journey to a fixed place and moves toward a more liberating notion of life as limitless becoming, endless possibility.

This study then moves to chapters on Ishmael Reed's *Flight to Canada* (1976) and Sherley Anne Williams's *Dessa Rose* (1986), both of which imagine the open journey as artistic creation. For each writer, slavery persists in modern times not only in economic and social terms but also in the "stories" imposed upon black people by white writers who either consciously or inadvertently present visions of the slave past that fix blacks in stereotypical roles. Liberation from this enslaving discourse is a two-part process for the black writer: (1) deconstructing fictions presented in works such as Stowe's *Uncle Tom's Cabin* and Styron's *The Confessions of Nat Turner*, which portray black history in flatly static terms; and (2) reconstructing new visions of the slave past from a fresh black perspective that envisions history as a fluid set of possibilities rather than a rigid set of givens, an open rather than a closed journey. For Reed, the act of writing itself creates the imaginative space he needs to "unwrite" *Uncle Tom's Cabin* and then create a fictive world in which his heroes can "write" their own identities in open, protean terms. "Canada" for Reed, therefore, is a free space in the mind rather than an actual place on a map; it is an open journey to new conceptions of self that the writer creates, not a fixed identity grounded in the stereotypical and racist assumptions found in well-meaning but racist texts such as *Uncle Tom's Cabin*. Williams clears a similar place for blacks in *Dessa Rose*, which aggressively deconstructs Styron's *The Confessions of Nat Turner*, a novel that imagines black history as a cycle of defeat and despair. Williams's book, brilliantly signifying upon black slave narratives and post–Civil War autobiographies, provides a counterdiscourse to Styron's novel by telling the story of its central characters' open journey West toward new lives and fresh possibilities.

The concluding chapter of this book focuses on Octavia E. Butler's *Parable of the Sower*, a novel that takes the African American journey motif one step further by projecting it literally into the future. By using a science fiction mode that very few black writers have shown much interest in, Butler provides new variations on the open journey, all the while infusing it with social and political themes that are relevant to contemporary life. While clearing new space for African American journey literature, she also connects her vision to a long tradition dating back to the spirituals and slave narratives. *Parable of the Sower*, while set in the twenty-first century, is a new kind of escape narrative in which enslaved people undertake an epic journey to the North in search of a mythic promised land, a fresh space promising new life.

This study of nine African American journey novels from the end of the Great Depression to the present day reveals an important change in the direction of modern black literature. Whereas earlier texts such as *Native Son* and *Invisible Man* valorize what Robert Stepto has described as "highly individualized mobility"[35] by celebrating physical and psychological journeys of radically isolated individuals who break away from all social constraints, more recent novels by Morrison, Reed, Johnson, Williams, and Butler make it clear that the open journey can be consistent with a vision of life that is social in nature. Williams's characters engage in the cooperative enterprise of a group of friends and family moving to the West to establish a new society. In the same way, Morrison, Reed, Johnson, and Butler imagine journeys that are more important for their cultural implications than their value for isolated individuals. Reed's novel attempts to reenvision black history to establish black culture in such a way as to ensure its growth. *Song of Solomon* imagines an epic journey to recover crucial truths about the black past that can serve as a force that brings black people together in a vital community that is always moving forward, having freed itself from the crippling myths of the dominant culture. *Faith and the Good Thing*, like Johnson's more recent fictions, is finally about the central character's desire to discover a potent myth that will reconnect the individual to a society that is constantly growing, moving towards new conceptions of self and community. And both *Dessa Rose* and *Parable of the Sower* portray journeys in which individuals form groups as they travel in search of a "new life" that consists not only of personal growth but also of social transformation.

The author wishes to thank the Mid-America Studies Association for permission to reprint parts of my article, "Down from Slavery: Invisible Man's Descent into the City and the Discovery of Self," *American Studies* 29, no. 2 (fall, 1988): 57–67. I also wish to thank the editor of *African American Review* for permission to reprint my article, "Making a Way Out of No Way: The Open Journey in Alice Walker's *The Third Life of Grange Copeland*," *Black American Literature Forum* 23, no. 1 (spring 1988): 44–79.

1

Stunted Picaresques: Zora Neale Hurston's *Their Eyes Were Watching God* and Richard Wright's *Native Son*

> I headed North, full of a hazy notion that life could be lived with dignity.
>
> —Wright, *Black Boy*

> The stuff of my being is matter, ever changing, ever moving, never lost.
>
> —Hurston, *Dust Tracks on a Road*

Zora Neale Hurston's *Their Eyes Were Watching God* (1937) and Richard Wright's *Native Son* (1940), seminal texts in the African American literary tradition, dramatically illustrate a problem often found in black fiction written before World War II. Although their central characters are strongly driven by the desire for open motion that characterizes the American picaresque tradition, they are frustrated by environments that block this drive. As a result, both novels take the form of what might be called "stunted picaresques," wherein the open journey is expressed as a metaphor that reveals the central character's deepest promptings and measures his or her inward growth but cannot be given full narrative form. In this way, these two novels illustrate a problem that goes to the heart of the black American experience in the twentieth century. Given a society that defines itself as open and fluid but attempts to systematically trap blacks in roles that severely limit their field of action, how do blacks gain access to an American Dream that is often portrayed in our classic literature as an open journey to unlimited possibilities? How do blacks make a way out of no way? *Their Eyes Were Watching God* and *Native Son* analyze this problem brilliantly

23

and begin to suggest ways of transcending it that subsequent black writers have explored fruitfully in a great variety of ways.[1]

The first paragraph of Hurston's novel establishes a polarity between stasis and open movement that is carefully sustained throughout the novel to express its central themes. Human aspiration and growth are suggested by lyrical images of free movement in open space, "ships at a distance" that "sail forever on the horizon," symbolizing "every man's wish." In sharp contrast, the stationary "Watcher" on shore is "mocked to death by time," turning his eyes away in "resignation."[2] The scene that immediately follows makes a similar contrast, counterpointing Janie Crawford's vital movements with the townspeople's stagnancy. Whereas she energetically moves down the road, the townspeople are described as "sitting on porches beside the road as they idly gossip about Janie." They are presented as numbed and inert, reduced to the status of "Mules and other brutes" (5) but Janie is depicted as energetic and alive, her "firm buttocks," "pugnacious breasts," and "great rope of black hair swinging to her waist" giving clear evidence of her "strength" (5). What the town resents most about Janie is her physical and social mobility, her refusal to "stay in her class," her habit of "runnin' after young boys" (5), and her leaving the town with Tea Cake Woods in pursuit of a new life in the larger world of Jacksonville and the Everglades. Envious of her free and unconventional life with Tea Cake, which serves as an indictment of their own stuffy and sedentary ways, they seek to stereotype her, labeling her as a fallen woman and reducing her to the status of an outsider with the "killing tools" (5) of their laughter.

Throughout the novel Janie's vitality is conveyed by her instinctive desires for open motion in free spaces not provided by the town, a monumentally static place intent on imprisoning her with conventional values and restrictive social roles. As a young girl Janie is fascinated by open space and motion. Her lively imagination is stirred by the horizon as she gazes at it in wonder and by the road that passes by the gate in her front yard. We are told that "Her conscious life had commenced at Nanny's gate" (13) when a young boy named Johnny Taylor came down the road and kissed her, bringing about an "end to her childhood" (14) and initiating her movement into womanhood. When her grandmother arranges a marriage between Janie and an older man named Logan Killocks to "protect" her from young men like Johnny Taylor and the larger world from which he comes, Janie develops the habit of standing near the gate, looking down "the road towards way off" (25), longing for the indefinite space and open movement that her marriage has denied her. Trapped in a dead relationship and a society that does not permit her to grow, Janie sustains herself by imaginatively contemplating images of motion and growth:

> So Janie waited a bloom time, and a green time and an orange time. But
> when the pollen again gilded the sun and sifted down on the world she
> began to stand around the gate and expect things. What things? She didn't
> know exactly. Her breath was gusty and short. She knew things that no-
> body had ever told her. For instance, the words of the tree and the wind.
> She often spoke to falling seeds and said, "Ah hope you fall on soft
> ground," because she had heard seeds saying that to each other as they
> passed. She knew the world was a stallion rolling in the blue pasture of
> ether. She knew God tore down the old world every evening and built a
> new one by sun-up. (24)

Janie's inward life is richly nourished by such images of motion and growth.
The drifting pollen, falling seeds, and galloping horses remind her that life
is a protean process that is always renewing itself, replacing the "old world"
daily with new forms of experience. For this reason Janie is especially
fascinated by the "blossoming pear tree" (13) in her backyard, seeing it as
a "revelation" of how the world is always changing, renewing itself in
motion:

> She was sitting on her back beneath the pear tree soaking in the alto
> chant of the visiting bees, the gold of the sun and the panting breath of the
> breeze when the inaudible voice of it all came to her. She saw a dust-
> bearing bee sink into the sanctum of a bloom; the thousand sister-calyxes
> arch to meet the love embrace and the ecstatic shiver of the tree from root
> to tiniest branch creaming in every blossom and frothing in delight. So
> this was a marriage. She was summoned to behold a revelation. (13)

Janie, like the tree, is outwardly still but inwardly teeming with movement
as her sexual nature is awakened by a "revelation" of bees penetrating blos-
soms and the entire tree is caught in an "ecstatic shiver" from its roots to its
branches. The life force is revealed to her as erotic movement culminating
in the tree "creaming in every blossom" and "frothing in delight."

If Janie's dynamic inward life is dramatized with such evocative images of movement and space, her outward life is usually described in terms
of indoor places that physically trap her and emotionally numb her with
stale routine. For example, all of the houses in which she lives are virtual
prisons. Her grandmother's house with its "narrow hallway" (14) and sick-
room is contrasted with the outside world with its "tree in bloom," "kissing
bees" (14), and open road. While the constant movement of the natural
world touches Janie's deepest longings, "Nothing in her grandma's house
answered her" (14). The house that she shares with her first husband is
even worse, "a lonesome place like a stump in the woods which is absent

of flavor" (21). Logan Killocks is exactly right when he accuses Janie of not taking "a bit of interest in this place" (29), for such an isolated, grim location is an objective correlative to their loveless marriage, which separates Janie from the vital realities that spur her growth. Her second husband, Jody Starks, promises her a more fulfilling life with "horizon" and "change" (28), but he provides her with an even more suffocating marriage, which is again symbolized by a house that imprisons Janie. The house that she shares with Jody is surely more opulent than those provided by her grandmother and Logan Killocks, but it too reduces her to the level of a slave. Jody, who firmly believes that a woman's "place is in de home" (39), builds a "gloaty, sparkly white" (42) home resembling a plantation "big house" (42) surrounded by smaller houses resembling slave quarters. Enslaved by the role of the mayor's wife who is expected to look pretty and submit to her husband's every wish as he pursues his career of politically and economically dominating the town he has created to serve his ego, Janie feels that she is little more than a piece of furniture in Jody's house. It is little wonder, therefore, that she comes to personify death as inhabiting a gigantic house:

> So Janie began to think of Death. Death, that strange being with the huge square toes who lived way in the West. The great one who lived in the straight house like a platform without sides to it, and without a roof. What need has death for a cover, and what winds can blow against him? He stands in his high house that overlooks the world. Stands watchful and motionless all day with his sword drawn back, waiting for the messenger to bid him to come. Been standing there before there was a where or a when or a then. (72)

Like many American and African American heroic figures, Janie equates death with stasis, a grim figure standing "motionless" in a house, and she equates life with movement, trees blooming, bees buzzing, and people ambling down an open road.

This dramatic contrast between Janie's dynamic inward life and her static outward existence produces a profound split in her character. Pulled in opposite directions, she develops two selves, "an inside and an outside," which she is careful not to "mix" (63). Her outside self requires her to present a "starched and iron face" (75) to a social world that expects her to "smile," even though she feels "stone dead from standin' still" (71). But her inside self is kept alive by her desire for movement—which is fulfilled in the second half of the novel when Tea Cake appears out of the road running in front of Jody's house and offers her a new life characterized by flight from conventional society into various forms of open space. While she senses "something dead" (67) in Jody and fears that their marriage has brought her to a "rut in the road" (66) that will emotionally cripple her, she sees Tea Cake as a picaresque figure whose constant ramblings will revive her because they inspire her own desires for movement and growth. Tea Cake initiates "her great journey to the horizons in search of people" (76) while Jody provides her with an existence that is characterized by "run[ning] off down a back road after things" (77). Tea Cake opens the "door" (131) to her inward life while Jody traps her in an outward life reducing her to the level of a "whipped . . . cur dog" (77).

Janie's life therefore can be seen as centered in two radically opposed journeys, a closed journey to restrictive places and an open voyage to liberating spaces. While the former is directed by others as they manipulate Janie's outer self, the latter arises from the deepest levels of her inward self as it is inspired by her own imagination and nourished by Tea Cake. Janie's grandmother, in her attempt to be "always guidin' [Janie's] feet from harm and danger" (15), forces her into a stultifying marriage to Logan Killocks, whom Janie envisions as "some ole skullhead in de graveyard" (15). The marriage, which her grandmother hopes will provide Janie with financial security and a stable home that will protect her from the ravages of a racist society, in fact enslaves her in gender roles that Logan's sexist consciousness imposes on her. He refuses to allow her to have any meaningful contacts in the larger world beyond home and makes her into a domestic slave who will cook his meals, chop his wood, and even help him to move manure piles. Janie decides to run away from him when he makes plans to force her to plow his sixty acres, harnessing her to a mule and, indeed, treating her like a mule. Jody Starks promises to release her from such drudgery, offering her an apparently freer, more spacious life as a middle-class wife of the town mayor, but he soon directs her movements in an equally authoritarian way. Like Killocks, who enslaves Janie to a place that suffocates her inward life, Jody stifles Janie by forcing her to play a subordinate role in his great plan to create an all-black town that he can rule over as absolutely as he presides over his marriage. Firmly believing that "She's uh woman and her place is in de home" (39), he reduces her to the same marginal status inflicted upon her by Killocks, forcing her to cook his meals, clean his house, and tend his store. Their marriage is appropriately captured in the image of her following silently behind Jody as the two return home from a political meeting in which he has forbidden her to speak:

It must have been the way Joe spoke out without giving her the chance to say anything one way or another that took the bloom off of things. But anyway, she went down the road behind him that night feeling cold. He strode along invested with his new dignity, thought and planned out loud, unconscious of her thoughts. (39)

Janie's relationship with Tea Cake offers her a radically different life with greatly expanded possibilities because he is the only person in the novel who lives outside the dictates of the "town mind" (42) and encourages her to break free of restrictive places and experience her life as an open journey through indeterminate space. From the outset he is depicted as a picaresque figure identified with free movement, appearing as he does out of nowhere and walking down the road that has inspired Janie's dreams of a new life. Well traveled, he gets around in a "battered car" (91) and does not hesitate to ride the rods of fast-moving trains when he lacks the money to move in more respectable ways: "When ah takes uh notion ah rides anyhow—money or no money" (83). Unlike her other two husbands, whom she imagines in static terms as weights that will physically immobilize her and emotionally kill her, she pictures Tea Cake in terms of constant motion in open space. For example, after they have made love for the first time she thinks of him as a free spirit moving in a fluid, indeterminate world:

> She could feel him and almost see him bucking around the room in the upper air. After a long time of passive happiness, she got up and opened the window and let Tea Cake leap forth and mount to the sky on a wind. That was the beginning of things. (91)

Whereas Killocks, whom she sees as a cadaver, and Starks, whom she envisions as having a "stillness in the back of his head" (67), encase Janie in a public self that is trapped in sterile routine, Tea Cake frees her by releasing her inward self, giving it "air," "sky" and "wind." In their first meeting his playful conversation with her triggers feelings she has not experienced since Johnny Taylor kissed her nineteen years earlier. As a result, "she found herself glowing inside" (81). They establish a private relationship apart from the town that nourishes her feelings and stirs her imagination, as he becomes her "great secret she was keeping from the town" (86). Falling in love with Tea Cake, Janie recovers the space that her grandmother had taken from her and she freely moves in that space. Realizing that "Nanny had taken the biggest thing God ever made, the horizon" (77) she ultimately resolves to live a free life that *she* directs: "Ah done lived Grandma's way, now ah means to live mine" (96).

Tea Cake helps to make this possible because he enables her to enter the open space that her inward nature has always craved. He not only teaches her to drive a car and brings her to the larger world outside the town—places such as Jacksonville, Ft. Meyers, and Ft. Lauderdale—but also brings her to the Everglades, a vast frontier that provides her for the first time in her life with an outward world that is as spacious as her inward life. Her "goin' off somewhere" with Tea Cake to "start over" (96) allows Janie to experience the human growth categorically denied by the places she has previously lived in and links her strongly to picaresque heroes in American and African American literary tradition who also achieve new lives by separating from social places and moving in radically open spaces.

From the very beginning Janie sees the Everglades as Natty Bumppo pictures the West or as Frederick Douglass imagines the North—as a fertile new space cut off from a confining past and offering new growth:

> To Janie's strange eyes, everything in the Everglades was big and new. Big Lake Okechobee, big beans, big cane, big weeds, big everything. Weeds that did well to grow waist high up the state were eight and often ten feet tall down there. Ground so rich that everything went wild. Volunteer cane just taking the place. Dirt roads so rich and black that half a mile of it would have fertilized a Kansas wheatfield. Wild cane on either side of the road hiding the rest of the world. People wild too. (107–8)

In "the trackless ways of the 'Glades" amid "the great sprawling Okechobee" (108) Janie is indeed separate from "the rest of the world" and can cast off the restrictive social roles and conventional values that have stifled her imagination and repressed her emotions. Whereas her marriage to Jody has "squeezed and crowded" (74) her spirit, her relationship with Tea Cake opens her mind and allows her to grow in many new ways. She learns how to shoot a rifle and spends a great deal of time in the wilderness hunting and fishing. She and Tea Cake share gender roles, with him often cooking breakfast and Janie working the bean fields; she greatly prefers such an active life to "settin' around the Quarters all day long" (111). In a world populated by "permanent transients with no attachments" (109) rather than townspeople mired in conventional roles condemning them to endless routine, she comes in contact with many folk cultures that deepen her consciousness and give her a new sense of pride in being a black woman. She enjoys the music and dance of the Bahamian migrants, as well as the blues and folktales of her fellow blacks. Looking back to her previous life in "the big white house in Eatonville" (111) she feels relieved to be away from such a stagnant environment.

Significantly, her life with Tea Cake in the Everglades allows her to actually experience the movement and growth that she could only imagine as a young girl:

> He could be a bee to a blossom—a pear tree blossom in the spring. He seemed to be crushing scent out of the world with his footsteps. Crushing aromatic herbs with every step he took. Spices hung about him. He was a glance from God. (90)

Whereas Janie as a young girl could thrill to the image of a pear tree blossoming, she now metaphorically becomes a blossoming pear tree, fertilized by Tea Cake's movements. Whereas she was never allowed to know people like Johnny Taylor who walked down the road, a "glorious being" moving through "pollinated air" (14), she now is married to a person whose movements down the road of life create aromatic "scent" to consecrate their relationship. Tea Cake also becomes the seeds that Janie beheld in wonder as a child—he tends a garden with her and after he dies she keeps only one of his possessions, the garden seeds he has bought to plant in the spring, because they "reminded Janie of Tea Cake more than anything else" (157–58).

Although Hurston is careful not to idealize or sentimentalize the Everglades as a Garden of Eden and stresses many of its negative features, such as its violent storms and occasionally violent human behavior, she does emphasize that the Everglades has nourished Janie more than any other setting she has lived in. Even at the peak of the hurricane that claims Tea Cake's life and nearly kills her, she reveals that she greatly prefers life in the Everglades with him than her life in the "big house" (130) that Jody had built. Living in the free spaces of the Florida swamps, Janie can experience new kinds of freedom, independence, and mobility, which give her a fresh conception of herself and the world. As she tells Tea Cake late in the novel, their relationship in the Everglades has saved her from the confusion and restriction of her previous life: "Ah was fumblin' round and God opened de door" (131). Once out into open space, they can position themselves in a manner where "They seemed to be staring at the dark but their eyes were watching God" (131).

It is important to realize, however, that *Their Eyes Were Watching God* does not end in the manner of classic American journey narratives that envision the central character experiencing a complete conversion to a new life and altogether transformed by open space. Unlike Natty Bumppo, who becomes more heroic as he moves further west into the uncorrupted frontier, and unlike Huckleberry Finn, who forever escapes the severe restrictions of conventional society by lighting out for the territories that promise him many new lives, Janie finally leaves the Everglades and returns to the town, which renews its fierce desires to discredit her and put her in her "place." Because she has associated Tea Cake so closely with the Everglades, she can no longer bear to live there after his death. Furthermore, her incarceration and trial at the end of the novel convince her that the patterns of racism and sexism that have restricted her previous life are not absent from even remote regions such as the Everglades. The racist whites who bring her to trial and the sexist blacks who cry out for her conviction for a crime she did not commit are ominous reminders to her that her "horizons" can be threatened wherever she is. She therefore returns to a town intent on punishing her and a house that has been her prison.

It would be a mistake, however, to conclude that Hurston's novel ends in despair, focusing upon a central character who has been defeated and forced to accept the role allotted to her by her grandmother at the beginning of the novel when she told her that "De nigger woman is de mule uh de world" (16). Janie's journey with Tea Cake to the Everglades has radically changed her, empowering her to return to Eatonville a very different person from the woman who was married for twenty years to Jody Starks. As Janie tells Pheoby at the outset of the novel, "Ah been a delegate to de big 'ssociation of life" (10), and her experiences in the Everglades have resulted in what the narrator calls "self revelation" (10). Although Janie's outward life will be severely limited by the town, her inward life has been enriched to the point that it provides a viable alternative to the town's rigidly stereotypical treatment of her. She is no longer the little girl who can be dominated by people like her grandmother or a young woman who can be controlled by men like Logan Killocks and Jody Starks. Whereas for much of her early life she had no satisfactory answer to the question whites put before her at age six—"don't you know yo' ownself?" (12)—at the end of the novel she is in firm possession of herself and can establish her identity by telling her own story. She therefore emphatically disproves her grandmother's warning that she cannot "stand alone by yo'self" (17). For her journeys have endowed her with inward resources that enable her not only to know herself but also to boldly assert herself, rejecting the dehumanizing roles and false values that others seek to impose on her.

Their Eyes Were Watching God, like so many African American novels written before World War II, is a stunted picaresque that ends ambiguously with the central character's situation defined with a complex mixture of images of stasis and motion. Janie senses this when she tells Pheoby at the end of the novel,

Ah'm back home again and Ah'm satisfied tuh be heah. Ah done been tuh de horizon and back now. Ah kin set heah in mah house and live by comparisons. Dis house ain't so absent of things lak it used tuh be befo' Tea Cake come along. It's fulla thoughts, 'specially dat bedroom. (158)

The novel's final meaning rests in what Janie calls "comparisons," the dialectical interplay of images of stasis and motion. Outwardly limited by the house that has formerly been her prison and the stifling society of "sitters and talkers" (158) who deny Janie's human complexity by fixing her in rigid stereotypes, Janie is nevertheless inwardly freed by the "horizon" she has recovered through her journeys. Her travels have set her mind and spirit in motion because they have taught her that love is not a "grindstone" reducing people to inert particles but is instead a "movin' thing" that is "lak the sea" (158). Love for Janie is a dynamic force always assuming new forms, always moving in unpredictable ways, and transforming the world, making it new each day.

The novel therefore concludes with an image possessing complexly double meanings, describing Janie as having "pulled in her horizon like a great fish net" (159). Although she is no longer a young girl who can look at the "never-landing" (5) ships on the open horizon and see them as a symbol of her own limitless possibilities, neither does she consider herself as "netted" or trapped. Because *she* now performs the act of netting, it no longer is an image of entrapment but has become an image of harvest. "Netting" her own living experience with her narrative, which she shares with Pheoby, she can convert girlish dreams into mature art that stimulates human growth. Hearing Janie's narrative, Pheoby exclaims: "Ah done growed ten feet higher from just listenin' tuh you, Janie" (158). Janie's continued growth is also stimulated as she "call[s] in her soul to come and see" (159) the vital horizon that her own art has caught wriggling in its meshes. Janie's story therefore comes to a bittersweet end—denied an outward frontier when she leaves the Everglades and returns to Eatonville, she is in the process of moving to the frontiers within her. Outwardly stilled by a society characterized by sexism and racism, she is inwardly alive, moving significantly through the considerable interior spaces that her journeys have opened up for her.

Richard Wright's *Native Son* also is a stunted picaresque because it too employs the open journey as a metaphor that expresses its central character's deepest yearnings; but it stops short of giving full narrative form to the open journey to reflect accurately the harsh realities of African American experience. While a rural society prevents Janie Crawford from fully experiencing her life as an open journey, Bigger Thomas is victimized by the systematic racism of the northern city. The white world is portrayed as a background threat in *Their Eyes Were Watching God*, hovering over the central character and making itself visible only when her movements bring her into the spaces that the dominant society has forbidden blacks to enter, but in *Native Son* white racism is always in the foreground of Bigger Thomas's experiences, tantalizing him with provocative images of open motion that evoke his most human longings and then frustrate those longings by trapping him in a smouldering ghetto that gives him daily evidence of how his culture limits his movements and desires.

This is clearly shown in an early scene in which Bigger and his friend Gus hang out on a street corner and observe the life around them:

> Bigger took out a pack and gave Gus a cigarette; he lit his and held the match for Gus. They leaned their backs against the red-brick wall of a building, smoking their cigarettes slanting white across their black chins. To the east Bigger saw the sun burning a dazzling yellow. In the sky above him a few big white clouds drifted. He puffed silently, relaxed, his mind pleasantly vacant of purpose. Every slight movement in the street evoked a casual curiosity in him. Automatically, his eyes followed each car as it whirred over the smooth black asphalt. A woman came by and he watched the gentle sway of her body until she disappeared in a doorway. He sighed, scratched his chin and mumbled,
> "Kinda warm today."[3]

Bigger's entire life is telescoped in this startling epiphany. While his altogether American longings are triggered by images of movement that define a world of change, growth, and possibility, his immediate social environment traps him, forbidding him access to experience that would respond to his deepest desires.

Just as Janie Crawford is imaginatively stirred by images of space and movement, the horizon and road that she gazes at on a daily basis, Bigger is touched at the core of his being by images of free movement—clouds "drifting," cars speeding over asphalt, and a woman gracefully moving down the street, her body moving in a "gentle sway." When Bigger then turns his gaze upward and sees an airplane skywriting the word "USE" (19), he beholds an objective correlative to his most profound desires, for he would like to "use" his life to "fly," literally becoming an aviator and figuratively achieving the social mobility promised by the American Dream. Gazing at the plane in "childlike wonder" (19), Bigger exhibits all of the most important characteristics of the Afro-American picaro, equating open movement with the possibility for a new life.

But like Janie Crawford who must view images of motion and space from behind a closed gate, Bigger is immediately reminded of the restrictions of the social world in which he lives. When he and Gus observe the movements of the protean world around them, they rest against a "red-brick wall" (18) that symbolizes the fact that American society has barred them from getting actively involved with such a growing, changing world. As Bigger gazes in wonder at the moving airplane, the narrator draws our attention to "the world of steel and stone," the "hard and mechanical" (19) environment that prevents Bigger from "flying." When Gus exclaims "Them white boys sure can fly" and Bigger replies "Yeah . . . They get a chance to do everything" (19), they formulate a powerful indictment of modern American society, which defines its basic values in terms of open space and free movement systematically denied to blacks.

As he looks at the world around him, Bigger is given daily reminders that he is trapped. For this reason, the novel is carefully structured as an elaborate sequence of scenes in which Bigger finds himself restricted in a variety of ways. The three major scenes in book 1—Bigger's killing of the rat, his near killing of Gus, and his accidental killing of Mary Dalton—are scenes of entrapment in which many kinds of environmental determinants restrict Bigger's consciousness and limit his free will, thereby forcing him into acts of reflexive violence that become more self-destructive as these scenes progress. Book 2, ironically subtitled "Flight," is also organized around three major scenes of entrapment. Bigger's murder of Bessie, his short-lived escape from the authorities, and his eventual capture portray him as compulsively repeating patterns of behavior brought on by environmental conditioning. Such repetition is continued in book 3, which is also centered in three major scenes that reduce Bigger to a state of incarceration—Bigger's conversation in his jail cell with friends and family, the dialogue between Max and Bigger in the visiting room, and his final talk with Max at the end of the novel. In each of these episodes Bigger is physically immobilized by a deterministic environment that will finally execute him.

Native Son, therefore, can be seen as structured as concentric circles wherein a racist environment systematically denies Bigger significant free will, gradually immobilizing him. As Wright revealed in "How Bigger Was Born," he intended the opening scene as a "type of concrete event that would convey the motif of the entire scheme of the book, that would sound, in varied form, the note that was to be resounded throughout its length, that would introduce to the reader just what kind of organism Bigger's was and the environment that was bearing hourly upon it" (xxix). In a sense, American society treats Bigger as the cornered rat that he kills in the opening scene, reducing him to a trapped animal that is killed because it is perceived as a threat to the social order. Just as the rat dies when Bigger smashes its head with a frying pan, Bigger dies when the state destroys him by attacking his head, hanging him until he is dead.

The pressures of a supposedly freer northern environment that paralyzes Bigger are even greater than the southern environment that seeks to immobilize Janie Crawford. The racist and sexist world that is intent on fixing Janie in dehumanizing roles does succeed in forcing her back to a house that has earlier served as a kind of prison, but it never stills her inward life, which is usually described as moving toward "horizons" that inspire her most human impulses. For much of *Native Son*, however, the social environment not only freezes Bigger into roles that greatly inhibit his outer movements but also cripples his inward life. The actual walls of the ghetto that force Bigger's family into a bare subsistence life in a one-room apartment eventually produce even more restrictive "walls" inside of Bigger's mind. As the narrator repeatedly tells us, Bigger tries to protect himself from a full awareness of his impotence in the outer world by retreating behind the thick walls that society has constructed inside his mind. This is established at the end of the novel's opening scene when Vera's moving behind a curtain to shield herself from view is linked with Bigger's moving behind a psychological wall:

> Vera went behind the curtain and Bigger heard her trying to comfort his mother. He shut their voices out of his mind. He hated his family because he knew that they were suffering and that he was powerless to help them. He knew that the moment he allowed himself to feel to its fullness how they lived, the shame and misery of their lives, he would be swept out of himself with fear and despair. So he held toward them an attitude of iron reserve; he lived with them but behind a wall, a curtain. And toward himself he was even more exacting. He knew that the moment he allowed what his life meant to enter fully into his own consciousness, he would either kill himself or someone else. So he denied himself and acted tough. (13–14)

Just as Vera's and Bigger's mother retreat behind a curtain to shield their personal distress from the view of others, Bigger represses his emotions behind a "wall" of acting "tough" so that others will not be aware of his vulnerability and pain. But he pays a terrible price for this because such walls not only separate him from others but also make it extremely difficult for him to experience the psychological and emotional growth necessary for him to challenge and overcome the demeaning roles and stereotypes imposed upon him. Unlike Janie who is outwardly trapped but inwardly free throughout her novel, Bigger is doubly trapped for much of *Native Son* and this leads him to commit acts of terrible violence that serve to intensify his fear and despair. Because he is both physically terrified of robbing Blum's store and emotionally afraid of revealing this fear to others, he assumes the protective role of tough guy, beating up Gus and almost killing him in the pool room. His self-destructive violence erupts on two other occasions: when he accidentally kills Mary Dalton and murders Bessie. In each of these scenes he is not only physically restricted in rooms that induce a sense of claustrophobia in him but he is emotionally trapped by the "walls" inside him that prevent him from expressing his feelings in a humane way. Mary's dark bedroom, with its walls that seem to close in on him, making him "afraid to move" (84), reflects the psychological walls that trap Bigger and make him feel "about to explode" from a "hysterical terror" that has "seized" him (84). In the same way, the cold walls of the abandoned building where Bigger rapes and kills Bessie are a mindscape reflecting Bigger's icy calculations to murder a person whom he is afraid to love.

While Bigger wants a life of motion symbolized by fast-moving cars, high-flying airplanes and romantic movies depicting dramatic "rises" in life, his trapped mind and body bring him to unsatisfying experiences such as working as a chauffeur who drives cars that others own and direct. The walls around him and inside him finally bring him to a dead halt in a prison cell that corners him in much the same way as the rat was trapped in the novel's opening scene. While the spirituals sung by his mother picture life as a "mountain railway" (14) to God or a speeding chariot carrying him "home" (77), the actual environment that Bigger confronts tries to rob him of significant motion. Many critics therefore have concluded that *Native Son* is a grimly naturalistic novel centered in a failed journey that reduces Bigger to purposeless drifting and culminates in his total paralysis. Blyden Jackson, for example, argues that

> At the end of *Native Son* the world of Bigger Thomas does not differ from what he has always known, a world in which, season in and season out, the elemental process is a holding action. . . . We know, at the end, that Bigger has made an effort to re-define his relationship with the world. We know that he has not succeeded in meaningful terms.[4]

In a similar way, Phyllis Rauch Klotman claims that Bigger's story ends in failure because he has made running not only a "criminal activity" but also a form of "psychic flight" that makes it impossible for him to develop a sense of self:

> Running *from* the self has only negative implications. It is an inversion of the pattern set by those nineteenth-century writers who were impelled toward new frontiers of awareness. An avoidance of knowledge, it is an escape that can only lead away from self-acceptance toward self-hate. Instead of an expansion of the self, we see in Bigger a shrinking from perception and a consequent diminution of the self.[5]

Jackson's interpretation needs qualification since it lays too much stress on the outward narrative of *Native Son*, which does indeed portray Bigger as helplessly trapped, and it does not take into account the novel's critically important inward narrative, an open journey to the self that allows Bigger to triumph in certain ways over his environment by developing a humane self. Klotman's interpretation of the novel, however, is a much more serious misreading, because it is at sharp variance with what the text emphasizes, especially in the second half of the novel. For while Bigger surely does run from the self in book 1 and the first half of book 2, hiding behind walls that obscure a humane vision of himself, he reverses this in the remainder of the novel, dismantling mental walls and courageously pursuing the truth of his life. Physically confined by city streets, abandoned buildings, a courtroom, and a jail cell, he nevertheless undergoes an important inward journey, one in which he follows a "strange path into a strange land" (107) of the inmost reaches of his thoughts and feelings. He thus takes "a new path" (142) in life and eventually finds a "road" leading him to a "sure and quiet knowledge" (226) of himself and his world. By the end of the novel he is shown as "groping forward with fierce zeal" (281) to a deeper knowledge of self that provides him with a new life as an existential hero rather than a naturalistic victim. Like Janie Crawford and the central characters of many other stunted picaresque novels, he is frustrated by his movements in external places but can move productively through his own inward spaces. Although this does not result in his transforming the outward environment, it does enable him to refuse to become what that environment wants him to be, a trapped rat. By the end of the novel Bigger is no longer the complete victim of environment who cried out "something's going to happen to me. . . . It's like I was going to do something I can't help" (24). Instead, he has gained a high degree of mastery over his inward life and can direct his actions in the outer world. His inward journey has empowered him to fashion a human self freed from the "walls" that have always imprisoned him and then move dramatically into new spaces of thought and feeling.

This inward journey has tentative beginnings in book 2 when Bigger runs away from the police and it develops fully in book 3 when he consciously deliberates over the meaning of his experiences. As Bigger escapes from the authorities after killing Bessie, his consciousness deepens and he is able to assert free will in several ways, even in the face of an environment growing progressively more hostile. He acquires a lucid vision of the world around him for the first time in his life and thus can begin to gain psychological distance from and emotional control over that world. In this way, he takes crucial steps toward selfhood, planting seeds that eventually flower in book 3. While trying to find his way through the labyrinthine streets of Chicago, for example, he obtains a new perspective on his life as a black American. When he climbs to the top of a tenement building and observes a black family living in a one-room apartment similar to that which he and his family rent and sees three black children in a bed watching their parents copulating, he thinks, "Five of 'em sleeping in one room and here's a great big empty building with just me in it" (231). Descending from the roof to secure food and warmth, he walks again through the streets, once more contemplating the social system that restricts blacks to impoverished ghettos: "They keep us bottled up here like wild animals" (233). Soon afterward, he spots "a big black rat" (233) leaping through the snow in search of a hole to protect it from the cold. In contrast to the novel's opening scene in which Bigger's frenzied emotions canceled out his conscious thoughts, reducing him to the level of the cornered animal that he kills, Bigger here retains a human identity by continuing to keep his emotions in check and thinking clearly. Shortly afterwards, he has another moment of sharp awareness when he goes to an abandoned building and observes from a window a religious service in an all-black church. Although the church is "dim-lit" (237), Bigger's mind is clearly illuminated by another significant insight: Conventional religion is another way in which black people are blinded to a social system that denies them a decent life. As he listens to the congregation singing "Steal away, steal away to Jesus," he consciously rejects this kind of "surrender, rejection" (237). Even though he is in certain ways attracted to the music because it provides him with a coherent vision of life that satisfies "his deep yearning for a sense of wholeness" (238), he honestly faces up to the fact that such a religious belief immobilizes them in the real world, encouraging them to accept injustice in the here and now by offering them a vaguely imagined happiness in a static afterlife.

Bigger's movements in book 2, while they do not result in his transcending the physical limits imposed upon him by his social environment, are successful because they awaken him intellectually, allowing him to destroy the walls inside him. As a result, he can move in book 3 to "the conviction that there was some way out" (256) of his trap, some "new mode of life" based upon a "new hope" (256). Like Janie Crawford, he becomes two selves, an outer self that is paralyzed and an inner self that has begun to move, steadily growing in a number of important ways. Strengthened by his new sense of self-worth, he attains psychological poise, "balanced on a hairline" (333), which enables him to mediate between the turbulent violence and numbing apathy described earlier as the two "rhythms of his life" (31). He can now center his life around a "thin, hard core of consciousness" (333) that helps him to transcend his earlier blindness and isolation, thus perceiving "vague relationships between himself and other people" that he has "never dreamed of" (334). Put another way, he feels "poised on the verge of action and commitment" (319) leading to genuine human growth.

To stress this human growth at the end of the novel, Wright dramatically reverses the meaning of key images used at the outset of the novel. Whereas Bigger's eyes are out of focus for much of the opening scene and he refuses to establish eye contact with people, in the final scene he looks directly at Max, whom he sees as "white, solid, real" (384). Whereas the harsh noise of the alarm clock in the first scene "galvanized" Bigger into "violent action" (8) in much the same way as Pavlov's dogs were mechanically stimulated by ringing bells, the clanging of his cell door described in the novel's final sentence produces in Bigger no outward motion but instead triggers an inward movement leading to a richly ironic awareness that he is psychologically freer and more emotionally alive than the novel's many blind people who continue to live as automatons driven by a mechanistic environment. Bigger's "faint, wry, bitter smile" (392), however, does not make him a hardened cynic like Buckley, who is incapable of sympathizing with or understanding other people. Bigger's smile is not only "bitter," suggesting his anger over human injustice, but also "faint" and "wry," suggesting a kind of objective awareness of human limitation. Bigger's facial expression therefore reflects the emotional complexity missing in the face described earlier in the novel, a face whose "clenched teeth" (8) reflected an animal consciousness linking Bigger to the rat he kills. Bigger's final words, moreover, are an attempt to reconcile himself with the people whom he had earlier hurt—he reassures Max that he is "all right" and asks Max to "tell Ma I was all right" (392). He also wishes to be remembered to Jan. Whereas Bigger was portrayed at the beginning of the novel as retreating behind mental walls and thinking that "the moment he allowed what his life really meant to enter fully into his consciousness, he would either kill himself or someone else" (14), he has now moved well beyond these walls, leading him to a new respect for himself and a concern for others. As a result, Bigger emerges from the novel as very different from the cornered animal he was in the opening scene. His physical movements have stimulated a journey to the open spaces of the self that transforms him.

The novel's most profound irony derives from the fact that the state executes Bigger precisely at this point where he is moving rapidly toward a liberating sense of self. Bigger's story, like Janie Crawford's narrative, therefore takes the form of a stunted picaresque that portrays the central character's open journey to the self but stops short of giving it full narrative form in outward experience. But *Their Eyes Were Watching God*, which ends significantly with the word "see" (159), and *Native Son,* which concludes with a related image of its hero gazing lucidly at a world he had earlier been blind to, establish a foundation in contemporary Afro-American fiction for fully picaresque novels that challenge and reinvigorate the tradition of American fiction with new forms of picaresque experience. Building upon and extending the modes of vision attained by Janie Crawford and Bigger Thomas, subsequent black writers like Ralph Ellison redefined the American open journey by dramatizing new ways of "seeing" and moving, thus making open movement one of the central motifs of contemporary African American literature.

2

Ralph Ellison's *Invisible Man:*
Exploring Urban Frontiers

The migrant masses, shifting from countryside to city, hurdle
several generations of experience at one leap, but more important, the same thing happens spiritually in the life attitudes and
self-expression of the young Negro, in his poetry, his art, his
education and his new outlook. . . . In the very process of being
transplanted, the Negro is being transformed.
—Alain Locke, "The New Negro"

Not only could you travel upward toward success, but you could
travel downward as well.
—Ralph Ellison, *Invisible Man*

At the end of the first chapter of *Black Boy* Wright makes a clear distinction between two kinds of picaresque journeys experienced by American
blacks in the twentieth century: the failed travels of men like his father,
who left his family to go North to escape responsibility, and the successful
odyssey that Wright himself experienced when he left the numbing South
to seek a protean identity in the North:

[M]y father was a black peasant who had gone to the city seeking life, but
who failed in the city; a black peasant whose life had become hopelessly
snarled in the city, and who at last fled the city—the same city which had
lifted me in its burning arms and borne me toward alien and undreamed-
of shores of knowing.[1]

Wright envisions his father's life as alternating in a futile way between
blank stasis and purposeless drifting, seeing him as a "creature of the earth"
who was "imprisoned by the slow flow of the seasons" in the South and

who made matters worse by wandering off to the North to be "hopelessly snarled in the city." But he regards his own life as radically different, declaring that he has been "swept . . . beyond" his father's life into redemptive urban space that expands his consciousness by providing him with "undreamed-of shores of knowing." The crucial difference between the two journeys, of course, is the consciousness of the traveler. While Wright's father was "chained" to his "direct, animalistic impulses," Wright was jarred by his "scalding experiences" into new modes of perception that enabled him to move purposefully from a static society to new spaces in the urban North that offered fresh possibilities of limitless growth.[2]

However much Wright saw his own life as an open journey, he was never able to construct a sustained fictional narrative to mirror adequately his own experiences. Many of his protagonists, like Fred Daniels of "The Man Who Lived Underground" and Cross Damon of *The Outsider,* resemble Wright's father, since they move away from restrictive societies only to be trapped in the alternate worlds into which they flee. And characters like Bigger Thomas experience life as a stunted, although not failed, picaresque journey. Even though their external travels stimulate open journeys within them leading to existential identities, they are unable to find adequate space in the actual world to sustain these new selves.

Ellison's *Invisible Man,* however, takes African American fiction a major step beyond stunted picaresques like *Native Son* and *Their Eyes Were Watching God* by centering upon a character whose deep and supple consciousness not only rejects the racist assumptions of American "place" but can transfigure such restrictive notions of place into a liberating space that can support a full and sustained open journey. The invisible man finally can use his intellect, will, and imagination to experience the modern American city as a new frontier rather than the Gothic mindscape that bewildered Bigger Thomas and the naturalistic trap that victimized Fred Daniels. And his underground room beneath city streets is radically different from the house to which Janie Crawford retreats at the end of her novel. Janie's house generates in her consciousness bittersweet memories—while her bedroom spurs thoughts of her liberating relationship with Tea Cake, the rest of the house is a grim reminder of her dead marriage to Jody and the restrictive domestic roles that the town would like to impose on her. The invisible man, however, has transformed his urban underground abode from a cold, dark place, a kind of a tomb, into a warm, bright space, a womb offering him new life and a new way of operating in the aboveground world. Because of this, his life has no end, only beginnings; it has become an open journey with limitless possibilities.

From the outset, *Invisible Man* is a novel that defines basic American and African American values in terms of the possibilities and limitations of motion. Its nameless hero is a wanderer who often identifies certain kinds of physical movement with moral and spiritual renewal. Like Melville's Ishmael, he never gives us the details that would help us to *place* him—a given name, a family past, or the exact spot in which he was born and raised.[3] Like Frederick Douglass, William Wells Brown, and many other African American picaros such as the protagonists of Claude McKay's *Home to Harlem* and Langston Hughes's *Not Without Laughter*, he concludes his narrative in an indefinite way. At the end of his novel he refuses to reveal exactly where he will go after he surfaces from his underground. His life, which is not tied down to any specific places or even an exact time, is notable for its constant change, movement, and freedom from rigidly fixed points of reference.

It is revealing too that he leaves for New York after being expelled from the college without carefully looking back at his past life. He never seriously considers returning home, nor does he initially tell his parents where he is going. The letter he eventually writes to them does not reveal the truth of his situation and his bouts of homesickness always pass quickly.

His entry into the city, therefore, recalls James Weldon Johnson's initial impressions of New York, and Langston Hughes's first moments in Harlem. In each case, the traveler feels altogether relieved to be freed from a restrictive place and contemplates in wonder the new possibilities of a liberating urban space. Wide-eyed with prospects of future happiness, invisible man quickly forgets any anxieties about being cut off from a stabilizing past or a familiar place. He dreams "with eyes blankly staring upon the landscape" as the bus approaches Manhattan.[4] Once in Harlem, he is intoxicated by the novelty, movement and pace of its life. The city as an actual place dissolves as his lively imagination transforms it into a world of fluid reality, endless opportunity:

> For me this was not a city of realities but of dreams; perhaps because I had always thought of my life as being confined to the South. And now as I struggled through the lines of people, a new world of possibility suggested itself to me faintly, like a small voice that was barely audible in the roar of city sounds. I moved wide-eyed, trying to take the bombardment of impressions. (122)

Late in the novel, he marvels about the northern city as a place where "You could actually make yourself anew" (377). Although he is disillusioned by many aspects of city life, he never loses this vision of the city as a dynamic process, a magical release from a confining mode of existence and the creation of new opportunities. With all its hectic movement and breathtaking fluidity, it is the complete antithesis of his stagnant life in the South. He never seriously disputes Peter Wheatstraw's claim that although Harlem "ain't nothing but a bear's den . . . it's the best place in the world for you and me" (133). Such a protean world is an extension of his fluid self, a personality that delights in novelty and constant metamorphoses.

In this way, *Invisible Man* is a striking reversal of many open journeys presented in mainstream American literature. Whereas one of the central drives in classic American journey texts such as *Walden*, "Song of Myself," *Death of a Salesman*, and *The Glass Menagerie* has been a nearly reflexive drive to move away from the complexity and supposed corruption of cities toward various types of pastoral settings, *Invisible Man* reduces to absurdity its hero's experiences in the rural South and extends to him the possibility of a kind of redemption in the northern city. The small town in which the hero grows up, ironically given the pastoral name of "Greenwood," is revealed in the Battle Royal episode as a place intent on blinding him with illusions about American life and trapping him in the debilitating roles of a segregated society. The college he attends appears to be a kind of "Eden" but is in fact a "flower studded wasteland" (29). The hero's experiences in both of these apparently bucolic settings arouse his hopes of finding a place for himself in the American dream but actually reduce him to the level of a robot controlled by people who use him for their own purposes.

His journey to New York, however, suggests a way out of these traps. After he has been "expelled" from his false Eden in the rural South and "cast into darkness" (105), he moves north to a larger and *potentially* more liberating world. What he must discover, however, is that the city that he beholds in such wonder is not a simple world containing one meaning but is in fact a tangle of painful contradictions. Like himself and American reality in general, the city is complexly double. He eventually realizes that "there were two of me" (281), a public self enslaved by society's expectation that he climb the ladder of outward "success" and a private self that is deformed by this "black rite of Horatio Alger" (87). In the same way, he comes to see New York as two mutually opposed cities: first, the city classically portrayed in Horatio Alger novels, an urban world enticing him with external rewards such as money, power, and status; and second, an existential city that offers an enriched consciousness leading to freedom and genuine selfhood.[5]

His movements in these cities take two very different forms. The Algeresque city invites him to move mechanically "upward" in American life toward various forms of outward success and a definite "place" in American society. But as the Battle Royal and his early experiences in New York clearly indicate, this upward movement exacts a terrible price, for it forces him to move away from the self toward various false roles eroding his identity. His movements in the existential city, however, are consistently *downward*, moving away from outward success and toward a greater degree of personal freedom, independence, and self-awareness. Rushing toward the center of Harlem late in the novel, he describes this movement as a race to the self: "I ran through the night, ran within myself" (403). And his self is described in existential terms as a fluid, open space that can be shaped and reshaped in limitless ways.

But for much of the novel he is engaged in a fruitless "footrace against" (287) himself as he moves blindly through an Algeresque city mapped out by others intent on using him. He is sent to New York by Bledsoe ostensibly to redeem himself after the fiasco at the Golden Day. His letters of recommendation to various important people in the city apparently will put him in touch with the "sponsors" who in the Alger myth always open the doors of success for the hardworking young boy desirous of "rising" in life.[6] The hero temporarily takes up residence in Men's House, a place that has traditionally housed black men who have left the South to pursue the American Dream in the North. But when he finds out from Emerson's son that his letters will not lead him to sponsors interested in helping him to "rise" in life, but, on the contrary, will put him on a wild-goose chase toward a "horizon" that "recedes ever brightly and distantly from the hopeful traveler" (145), he rejects everything that Men's House stands for and resolves to make his own way in the city.

Ironically, however, he uses another recommendation, the one provided by Emerson's son, and this brings him to Liberty Paint, which is described as a "small city" (149). What he encounters there is another version of the Alger myth that now promises upward mobility by becoming part of a complex industrial society. Here again, the city seems to offer freedom from a restrictive southern past but in fact provides him with another version of that past. Working for Kimbro, whom his fellow workers characterize as a "slave driver" (151) and whom he sees as "a northern redneck, a Yankee cracker" (152), he becomes part of an urban plantation that reduces him to the level of a sharecropper at best and a slave at worst. The hero is exactly right when he thinks that "there were unseen lines which ran from North to South" (128). Attaining one's freedom is not a simple matter of physically moving to a northern city, because this part of the urban North has been contaminated by the same racism and brutality that characterize the pastoral regions of the Deep South.

Even in his acts of conscious rebellion against the Alger myth the hero ironically repeats the experience of slavery in the northern city. Signing up with the Brotherhood because it promises him "the highest possible rewards" (268) and a liberating role to play, he ultimately discovers that he is trapped in the same way that he was trapped in the Battle Royal. Here again he is carefully monitored by whites who want to make him "the new Booker T. Washington" (231), a person who will channel black political energy into forms that are acceptable to whites. And just as his involvements in the Battle Royal result in self-destructive violence for himself and others, his involvement in the Brotherhood culminates in the Harlem riot that the Brotherhood engineers, a mad explosion that the hero ultimately describes as "not suicide but murder" (417). Put another way, his Brotherhood experiences lead him to yet another dead end, confinement in a Dantean "city of the dead" (324), a Hell brought on by his own blindness and desires for power and status.

What he needs to enter the existential city of possibility is the kind of consciousness necessary to correctly *read* his urban experiences so that he can map his own way through the city and thus discover the city as a reflector and liberator of the self. In the Vet's words, he has "to learn to look beneath the surface" (118). This ultimately brings him literally into an existential underworld that frees him by completely inverting the values of the Alger myth, sending him *down* to the liberating regions of the self instead of up toward the material goals that have in fact enslaved him all his life.

Getting to the urban underworld, however, is no easy process, because he has always been trained to see success in Algeresque terms as upward movement and freedom, or in Booker T. Washington's terms as rising from a condition of servitude. He begins the process of liberation leading to the "underground" of the self by spontaneously wandering through the hidden parts of the city, slowly becoming more aware of it as an emblem of the hidden parts of himself. Penetrating a city that he informally maps for himself, he gradually discovers the hidden open spaces of his own nature.

This process begins shortly after the hospital sequence in which he takes the subway to Harlem and then passes out on the streets. Stunned by the explosions at Liberty Paint and the electroshock therapy at the hospital, the hero is freed from the conventional "plan" for success imposed on him at the Battle Royal and reinforced in all subsequent episodes. Significantly, he moves to Harlem, which is a kind of underground, a "city within a city" (122). His free movements in Harlem repeatedly result in increased self-awareness as he discovers the falsity of an American Dream that promises freedom for all but creates an immense ghetto depriving enormous masses of their political, social, and economic rights. Developing the habit, while living with Mary Rambo, of reading books from the library during the day and "wander[ing] the streets until late at night" (197), the hero begins the slow process of reading the city and the self through an open journey in both external and internal worlds. Deciphering the codes contained in books and the urban landscape, he finally begins to interpret the secrets that have been deeply buried within himself for most of his life.

The first example of this occurs approximately halfway through the novel when, hurrying through the streets one day, he comes upon a vendor selling yams. This key episode endows him with "an intense feeling of freedom" (201) because it awakens in him a renewed respect for his folk traditions and their ability to "nourish" him more than the Alger myth, which has him rejecting soul food for a standard breakfast of toast, juice and coffee. The scene contrasts sharply with an earlier episode on the city streets when the hero meets the man calling himself Peter Wheatstraw. Whereas in the earlier episode, the hero was not able—and probably unwilling—to decipher the folk codes that are such a key part of his identity, here he understands what the street vendor is talking about and identifies strongly with the rich ethnic past that the sweet yams evoke. While the earlier street scene with Wheatstraw resulted in the hero rejecting his racial traditions, thinking "they're a hell of a people" (135), this scene in Harlem culminates in his thinking with pride "What a group of people we were" (200).

Shortly after this, he moves into a "side street" (202) where his perceptions are developed further as he witnesses an old black couple being evicted from their apartment. The vaguely felt nostalgia induced by eating the yams becomes a much more disturbing feeling of anger and betrayal when he sees all of the couple's possessions thrown out on the street, reduced to what he will later describe as "junk whirled eighty-seven years in a cyclone" (210). Again, the urban scene speaks to him in a vital way:

> I turned aside and looked at the clutter of household objects which the two men continued to pile on the walk. And as the crowd pushed me I looked down to see looking out of an oval frame a portrait of the old couple when young, seeing the sad, stiff dignity of the faces there; feeling strange memories awakening that began an echoing in my head like that of a hysterical voice stuttering in a dark street. (205)

Here the outer cityscape becomes a compelling metaphor of the hero's self, which is tied to a cultural and racial past for which he finally takes responsibility. As he observes the dispossession of the old couple, he realizes that he too has been dispossessed of the same American Dream promised to them. The outward street thus becomes the "dark street" of his mind, filled with a critically important new sign of selfhood, the "hysterical voice" so long repressed since the Battle Royal but which now cries out for full articulation.

Throughout the remainder of the novel the hero continues to move into the open spaces of the self as he freely explores the existential city. Wandering the streets after he has witnessed Clifton's death, he thinks: "It was as though in this short block I was forced to walk past everyone I had ever known" (335). More importantly, he becomes increasingly sensitive to two voices that he had previously been trained to ignore—the voice of the city and the voice arising from the deepest levels of his consciousness. From his very first moments in Harlem he had been aware that these two voices were somehow related:

> . . . I had always thought of my life as being confined in the South. And now as I struggled through the lives of people a new world of possibility suggested itself to me faintly, like a small voice that was barely audible in the roar of city sounds. I moved wide-eyed, trying to take the bombardment of impressions. (122)

Just as the constant movements and loud roar of the city awaken his sensations so that he sees and hears in an intensified way, they also release in him a "small voice" of possibility that was muffled in the Battle Royal episode and completely silenced in his interview with Bledsoe. The vital roar of the city, so unlike the deadly quiet of the campus, begins a true process of education for the hero because it draws from him the existential "voice" that is at the core of his self.

As the novel progresses, the hero's small voice amplifies as his consciousness of the city becomes more comprehensive and enriched. After delivering a Brotherhood speech, he thinks: "I threw my voice hard down against the traffic sounds" (278). While speaking at Clifton's funeral he imagines the crowd looking at "the pattern of my voice on the air" (343). By the end of the novel, he has developed a voice that is as richly complex and sophisticated as the city itself. Moreover, he has switched from an oral to a written voice, moving from the status of orator to novelist. This is a crucial change, for it makes him less dependent upon the needs of his immediate audience and better able to sound his own depths. The role of writer also grants his voice a greater degree of permanency and universality, enabling him to reach the "lower frequencies" (439) that speak to all people.

The invisible man, therefore, stops modeling himself on Norton, Bledsoe, the Founder, and others who deceived him with the Alger myth, and he ultimately sees himself as a latter-day Frederick Douglass, the man who liberated himself by undertaking an open journey from the rural South to the urban North and in the process created his own voice and identity. He admires Douglass as the man who "talked his way from slavery" (285) and created his own name, thus signifying the fact that he was a truly self-made man, one who became humanly successful, not by accumulating wealth and status but by fully actualizing the self. In this way, he rejects a superficial Algeresque plan for success and celebrates a more essential American dream, an existential version of Emersonian self-reliance.

In other words, the invisible man achieves a protean identity by rejecting his life as a closed journey that is directed to particular places that fix him in specific roles; instead, he embraces his life as an open journey in free space which assigns him "no rank or any limit" (435). Moved first from his hometown to an Alabama college by racist whites intent on driving him crazy, he then goes to New York, blinded by the fool's errand that Bledsoe has directed with letters of recommendation that reduce him to a joke. But once in New York he is transformed by the city's openness and constant movement, eventually moving into his own inward spaces.

In order to achieve the experience of his life as an open journey, he must carefully mediate between two extremes: stasis and purposeless movement. He is often threatened by two kinds of stasis: complete paralysis and mindless circularity, outward motion that really goes nowhere. Purposeless movements also take two forms: a random drifting and greatly accelerated activity that eventually goes out of control. Although he sees life as constant flux, the hero finally realizes that his experiences must have a loose but humanly satisfying design controlled by a flexible purpose and a tentative direction. While it is important to note that the hero's journey is not circumscribed by a particular place or a fixed meaning, it nevertheless is purposeful. An ongoing process of self-discovery, it finally leads to a fuller awareness of the complexities of his protean identity.

When the narrator loses control of his movements, he usually faces disastrous consequences. For example, he makes one of his major mistakes while aimlessly driving with Norton through the countryside. Taking the old man much too literally when he claims he would like to go "anywhere" (30), the hero drives off the highway, for no apparent reason, and down the dirt road leading to Jim Trueblood's house and the Golden Day. His random movements gradually accelerate, resulting in a whole series of bewildering and painful episodes that culminate in his being sent on a fool's errand to New York by Bledsoe. This absurd task does not end until he gains conscious control over his life while underground.

The Battle Royal confronts the narrator with all of these negative forms of motion and becomes, therefore, a central epiphany of what he should not do with his life. The scene itself is a grisly spectacle of chaotic movement, "complete anarchy" (19). Although the initial preparations might indicate a highly structured ritual, the actual results are a pandemonium of noise, terror, and hysterical motion—the boys blindly punching each other, the stripper trying to escape the "mad" (17) chase of the men who attempt to rape her, and people wildly scrambling after phony money. All this is acted out in a room that is a surreal "swirl of lights, smoke, sweating bodies" (19). Caught in this whirling nightmare, the hero realizes: "Blindfolded, I could no longer control my motions. I had no dignity" (18).

The final events of the Battle Royal, however, present the narrator with an equally inhuman alternative, paralysis. The speech he delivers is a statement about staying in his "place," a world drained of opportunities for real development. Plagiarizing Booker T. Washington's Atlanta Exposition Address, he says:

> To those of my race who depend upon bettering their condition in a foreign land, or who underestimate the importance of cultivating friendly relations with the Southern white man, who is his next door neighbor, I would say: "Cast down your buckets where you are." (24)

This argument for not moving out of the rural South, of course, is richly satisfying to his white audience because it guarantees them a cheap labor supply that has no clear ideas of genuine advancement. By keeping black people where they "are," southern whites can deprive them of their freedom.

Assured that the invisible man will "lead his people in the proper paths" (25), ending in a cultural dead end, they reward him with a briefcase and a scholarship to a Negro college. Both impel him on a false quest that is pointed toward his destruction. For the road to the college, as we soon find out, leads to the madhouse, a world that alternates between moral paralysis and occasional moments of insane physical movement at the Golden Day.

The briefcase, likewise, fills the hero with delusions of being "successful" in the white world and, as the vet later tells him, this also leads to madness.

Ellison artfully establishes the Battle Royal as a central episode that gets repeated in many different forms throughout the novel. Most of the hero's outward adventures, therefore, are a deadly circle of repetition that force him to relive the humiliations of this event in his late adolescence. The dream he has immediately afterwards is a clear prefiguration of this. In it, his grandfather opens the briefcase and finds a seemingly endless number of envelopes contained within each other, representing the "years" (26) of the hero's life. And they all express the same depressing message: "Keep this Nigger-Boy running" (26). Although it will take the narrator a long time to realize this, the life that white society has planned for him consists of a wild-goose chase ending in exhaustion and stasis.

His activities at the Golden Day are clearly another version of what has happened in the Battle Royal. In both scenes, he is a passive victim of an incoherent, violent, and quick-moving world that leaves him dazed and confused. Likewise, the fiasco at Liberty Paints depicts the eruption of a seemingly rational world into confused motion and incoherent violence that he can neither understand nor control. The scenes in the factory hospital that follow immediately induce the same kind of paralysis he experienced while giving his graduation address. And this speech, controlled by white people who manipulate him for their own self-interest, is a preview of most of the speeches he will give for the Brotherhood. Jack, who is intent on making him "the new Booker T. Washington" (233), monitors his talks as carefully as did the southern whites. Finally, the Harlem Riot at the end of the novel brings his actions full circle, enacting on a large scale the absurdities of his hometown. Here too, the central character is reduced to the status of a passive victim observing a scene of mad violence, raucous noise, and wild motion.

Most of the novel's major scenes utilize important images of circularity to further underscore the futility of the movements that they dramatize. The stripper from the Battle Royal dances in "graceful circles" (17) and Homer Barbee paces in a semicircle as he delivers his oration about the Founder. Both people are parts of rituals that they do not fully understand and blindly repeat for the sake of their audiences. As the hero drives Norton down the road to Trueblood's house, he observes birds circling overhead. He also sees "pigeons circling" (217) immediately before he runs into Jack during the eviction episode and he notices exactly the same image right before Clifton is killed. In all three cases, the circling of the birds is a foreshadowing of similar disasters—experiences that fly out of control because the hero fails to understand their nature. They prefigure the nightmare at the end of the novel in which he imagines himself being castrated by the various people who have run his life. Here too, a circular image is used to suggest the hero's helplessness—a butterfly is described as circling "three times around . . . [his] blood-red parts" (430).

The circle is also used to suggest the invisible man's inner confusion. As he smarts from Kimbro's criticisms at the Liberty Paint factory, his emotions are described as "whirling" (155). Similarly, in his final show-down with Jack he feels his own head is "whirling as though [he] were riding a supersonic merry-go-round" (357). The final result of his liaison with Sybil is to cut him loose from any center of gravity and to put his head "awhirl" (401). The terror and confusion inspired by the Harlem Riot is clearly depicted by the hero stumbling "in circles" (424) as he searches for Mary Rambo's apartment. (These scenes are technically unified by the diz-zying motion of the narration itself. Each episode is basically surreal and nervously paced, often giving the impression of having been filmed by a movie cameraman who rapidly pans his scenes and blurs his focus to give an artful effect of psychological disorientation.)

These sequences, therefore, define the hero's life prior to his move-ment underground as an iron circle of necessity that can be broken only if he becomes sufficiently aware of his situation. Although he shows some limited awareness of this by the novel's midpoint, such knowledge is eas-ily dissolved by the fast pace of events. For example, as he enters the Chthonian with Jack, he twice thinks "I had been through it all before" (228), but this vague perception does not add up to anything useful. While delivering his first Brotherhood speech, he also "felt the hard, mechanical isolation of the hospital machine" (258), but he fails to realize that the insane doctors at the hospital and Jack are virtually the same people. Ironi-cally, he sees his Brotherhood experiences as a liberating "new life" radi-cally separated from his past:

> This was a new phase, I realized, a new beginning, and I would have to take that part of myself that looked on with remote eyes and keep it al-ways at the distance of the campus, the hospital machine, the battle royal—all now far behind. . . . For if I were successful tonight, I'd be on the road to something big. (253–54)

Lulled by the illusion that the Battle Royal and related experiences are "far behind" him, he has little understanding that "the road to something big" is the same worn path that the southern whites had put him on as a reward for his graduation address.

Critics have often expressed dissatisfaction with the ending of *Invis-*

ible Man because they can discover no real basis for the affirmations that they feel the author intends. In an early review of the novel, Irving Howe, for example, argued that the hero's final discussion of his possibilities was unconvincing, since he did not specify their exact nature.[7] Likewise, Marcus Klein viewed the narrator's optimism in the epilogue as "desperate, empty, unreasonable and programmatic,"[8] since his journey is a depressing circle that has trapped him. Edward Margolies, in the same way, felt that the hero's affirmations at the end of the novel are ineffective because "there is no evidence in the text to fortify his beliefs."[9]

Other critics, therefore, have felt free to interpret the book in completely pessimistic terms. Floyd Horowitz claimed that the narrator's movements finally lead him "nowhere" and that "his self-imposed basement exile is therefore an escape from responsibility."[10] Roger Rosenblatt has described the narrator's travels as a complete reductio ad absurdum:

> As a romance, nothing is at the end of the quest; as a bildungsroman, nothing is the product of the education; as a tour de force, nothing is the vehicle. The hero progresses from South to North to nothing; from capitalism to communism to nihilism. He makes a long and arduous journey which ends in a basement. . . .[11]

More recently, Charles Johnson has observed in *Being and Race* that Ellison's protagonist has "nowhere to go except outside the lives of others, below the social world, which he lives off parastically."[12]

It is my purpose, however, to demonstrate that these views of the book are inadequate because they fail to account for either the author's intentions, the novel he wrote, or the traditions he operated in. The hero's journey, examined in these contexts, does have a positive meaning. The fact that the invisible man cannot finally tell us precisely where he will go does not imply that his journey is over and drained of meaning. Rather, it links him to many other American and African American heroes who are careful not to tie themselves down to specific journeys for fear that they will constrict their own possibilities. The fact that Huck Finn heads vaguely for the "Territory ahead" does not undercut the positive meaning of his journey but adds to it. Similarly, the indefinite placement of Whitman's hero at the end of "Song of Myself" underlines the extraordinary openness and fluidity of his experiences. The indeterminateness at the close of Langston Hughes's *The Big Sea*, likewise, suggests its author's faith in his abilities to transcend the tight strictures of a racist society and to pursue the myriad possibilities of his own life. In the same way, the spatially undirected nature of the hero's movements at the end of *Invisible Man* suggests that he has more than one life to lead. We must, therefore, take very seriously his claim that he will soon end his hibernation, shaking off "the old skin" (438) and become a new man.

His movement into the urban underground, far from being a cop-out ending in moral paralysis, is actually a temporary exile, what Frost has called "a strategic retreat,"[13] which will allow him to gain the kind of awareness that is a precondition to meaningful action. This is the sort of perspective that Leslie Fiedler has claimed is essential to the American experience because it has created a uniquely American consciousness:

> Fleeing exclusion in the Old World, the immigrant discovers his loneliness in the New World; fleeing the communal loneliness of the seaboard settlements, he discovers the ultimate isolation of the frontier. It is the dream of exile as freedom which has made America but it is also the experience of exile as terror which has forged the self-consciousness of Americans.[14]

Since his own withdrawal from outer reality results in precisely this mixture of existential freedom and terror, the hero can develop the "complex double vision"[15] that Ellison has claimed is necessary for both survival and success in African American life. Thus, the narrator's insistence in the epilogue that he is still able "to condemn and affirm, say no and say yes" (437) is much more than empty raving, "buggy jiving" (439).

Indeed, his flight underground provides him with a world that has real similarity with the frontier to which classic American heroes have moved. Ellison, who has taken great pains to define his own social background as western rather than southern,[16] consciously exploits the imagery of the West in defining his narrator's urban underground as an escape valve that still works. Just as in *Shadow and Act* he identifies his boyhood home as the "border"[17] state of Oklahoma, he places the invisible man in a "border area" (5) between Harlem and the larger white world. He also takes pleasure in having some of the Harlem rioters characterize Ras as a demented cowboy: "Ride 'em cowboy. Give 'em hell and bananas" (425). Then too, the hero's sense of his underground as "space, unbroken and impenetrable" (428) would suggest a clear parallel with the indefinite land areas classically associated with the West. Such a "dimensionless" (429) world gives him the psychological room he needs to imagine himself in fresh new ways. Although his coal cellar, like the West, was "shut off and forgotten during the nineteenth century" (5), his imagination can reopen it and make it live as a traditional symbol of American opportunity.

Such a world, therefore, is a brilliant modern equivalent of what Frederick Jackson Turner classically defined as "the meeting point between savagery and civilization."[18] Poised between the barbarous outer world of Ras the Destroyer and the richly cultivated life of his own mind, the hero can devise a mode of consciousness and action that will intelligently mediate between these extremes. He may, therefore, move productively inward to the self and outward to the social world. For his existence under the streets of New York is not the "underground" (347) in which Tod Clifton is buried, a condition of final stasis. Nor is it the bizarre "underground" (157) that traps Lucius Brockway in his illusions. Rather, it is an awakening process that endows him with vision (light) and power (electricity). As such, it ultimately enables him to move back into the external world with renewed confidence and ability. He is not "blind 'sa mole in a hole" (396) like Sybil's husband but a person in the process of undergoing the kind of metamorphosis that standard American heroes have experienced in the West, on the open road, or at sea. For once removed from the madly paced, disintegrating world of external events, he is able to understand that the chronic failure of his past consists of "trying to go in every way but my own" (433). This kind of self-reliance is the first step in charting his own way in the world.

What this way will be is never made exactly clear, nor could it be. For Ellison's central character sees his future in quintessentially American and African American terms, as a succession of open possibilities rather than a rigid sequence of events. Finally grasping the vet's claim that "the world is possibility if you'll only discover it" (120), he perceives his underground as part of an American process of renewal:

> Yes but what *is* the next phase? How often I have tried to find it! Over and over again I've gone up to seek it out. For, like almost everyone else in this country, I started out with my share of optimism. I believed in hard work and progress and action, but now after first being "for" society and then "against" it, I assign myself no rank or any limit, and such an attitude is very much against the trend of the times. *But my world has become one of infinite possibilities.* What a phrase—but still it's a good phrase and a good view of life, and a man shouldn't accept any other; that much I've learned underground. Until some gang succeeds in putting the world in a strait jacket, its definition is possibility. Step outside the narrow borders of what men call reality and you step into chaos—ask Rinehart, he's a master of it—or *imagination.* That too I've learned in the cellar, and not by deadening my sense of perception; *I'm invisible. not blind.* (435; italics added)

What is important here is that there will be a "next phase" and the hero has been aboveground many times to seek it out. Invisible but not blind, he understands that life in America may indeed be an endless series of next phases, indefinite possibilities for development. But this need not plunge him into Rinehart's world of "chaos," a morally purposeless, anarchic world that he has tried and rejected. There is an alternative to this, the liberating world of the imagination that can dissolve "the narrow borders of what men call reality" while creating a flexible kind of order to control the fluid reality that emerges. By expanding his perceptions rather than deadening them and by following the example of Louis Armstrong and other creators whom he admires, he may literally become an artist. For as Ellison has made clear in *Shadow and Act*, art is a basic way of controlling experience: "Life is as the sea, art is a ship in which man conquers life's crushing formlessness."[19] This is precisely the function of the blues that Peter Wheatstraw sings and the spirituals performed at Tod Clifton's funeral—to transfigure the pain of life's chaos by giving it organic, living shape. Clearly, this is also the function of the novel that the narrator gives us: to make sense of an apparently absurd world by submitting it to the discipline of art.

Or the hero may certainly choose other roles in the outside world—he could, for example, discover that there are political commitments more meaningful than those offered by either Ras or Jack. (The novel ends, after all, on the verge of the Civil Rights movement, which would drastically change the lives of American blacks.) Thus shaping his own life as the artist discovers the elusive organic form of his materials, he may break the dead circle of his past and move in positive new directions. Although he is surely correct when he finally tells Norton "Take any train; they all lead to the Golden Day" (437), he is no longer riding on the iron rails of other people's expectations. Instead, he has come to Frederick Douglass's realization that he may create his own road and travel on it in any number of directions.

Marjorie Pryse is therefore misleading when she claims that "The myth of the North is gone; Brother Tarp's physical flight to freedom is no longer an option for Invisible Man."[20] Ellison's protagonist gives this important African American myth new vitality by internalizing it and thus providing blacks with a twentieth-century Underground Railroad to inner freedom. Moreover, he also has faith that movement in the physical world is still a liberating prospect once one has achieved the supple consciousness to flexibly direct that movement. He promises to return to the fast-paced life of surface events, stressing that "Without the possibility of action, all knowledge comes to 'file and forget' and I can neither file nor forget" (437).

Since his underground makes possible both inward and outward movements, it frees him from the trauma of the Battle Royal. Consciously assimilating his past rather than crudely rejecting it or sentimentally idealizing it, he may move in new directions:

> And now I realized that I couldn't return to Mary's or to any part of my old life. I could approach it only from the outside, and I had been as invisible to Mary as I had been to the Brotherhood. No, I couldn't return to Mary's, or to the campus, or to the Brotherhood, or home. I could only move ahead or stay here, underground. (431)

Approaching his life in this way "from the outside," he can gain a mature perspective on it, using it as a way of illuminating his present and future experiences. He can thus avoid the brute circularity and randomness of his past movements. But he is clearly opposed to the idea of staying underground too long. The freedom he seeks is more than "simply the freedom not to run" (434); it is the freedom to move ahead purposely in life.

While rushing around for the Brotherhood, the narrator complains of his running a footrace "against" (287) himself. But late in the novel, as he speeds toward the Harlem riot that will disabuse him of many illusions about his identity, he imagines his experiences as a running "within" (403) himself. This crucial change is central to the novel because the hero's quest for identity can assume a fruitful direction only if he stops opposing his protean self with the fixed roles others have given him. Running against himself, he goes nowhere, but running *to* himself he may discover the way that leads "home," his identity as a black American. Although by the conclusion of the novel this important movement has really just begun and the hero is a long way from any definite end point, this is no cause for the despair that many critics have spoken of. Realizing that life is a dynamic process rather than a fixed journey, the hero's movements provide him with the mobility and loose direction that he needs. It finally places him in harmony with what his author has described as "the magical fluidity"[21] of American life.

Put another way, the novel finally transfigures the symbol of the circle, investing it with dramatically new positive meanings. Although most of the hero's life is portrayed as a deterministic circle whose circumference traps him and whose center evades him, he is ultimately able to see his life as a series of circles that radiate indefinitely outward from a coherent center. Unlike Norton, who will never get to Centre Street because he will always be trapped by the abstract designs that rigidly direct his life, Ellison's narrator does manage to find the core of his experiences and to work outward from there. Whereas Norton is attempting to get to the locus of city government in New York, thus tapping its "power," Ellison's hero is moving toward personal centers of strength, rejecting the public masks he has worn throughout the novel. In entering the underground, he goes *into* a circle after lifting the manhole, a "circle of holes in steel" (428). This solid and rigid circular object dotted with a number of small circles is clearly a symbol of the life that he has led up to this point. By penetrating it, he creates important new directions for himself, a centripetal journey to the self that will eventually enable him to move productively outward to the larger social world. Looking at the iron manhole and paying special attention to the various holes cut into it, he has a sudden revelation: "This is the way it's always been, only now I know it" (428). This realization that his life has been a series of repetitions embedded in the hard, tough substance of other people's plans for him is a major step toward freedom. Significantly, this epiphany is soon followed by the ritual burnings of the past identities contained in the briefcase he was awarded on the night of the Battle Royal. Having destroyed the betrayals implicit in his high school diploma, Clifton's doll, Jack's letter, and the Brotherhood's identity card, he concludes: "You've run enough, you're through with them at last" (429). The fool's errand initiated by the Battle Royal has come to an end.

Now that his underground life has generated a true consciousness, he is able to reject his earlier view of reality as mechanical sequence, linear progression. This is the meaning of his statement in the prologue that the world moves in the manner of a boomerang instead of an arrow. But this is not a solipsistic process that will trap the hero. The mind moving in these circles transforms experience by saturating it with consciousness. This in turn provides novel forms of thought and action. The circle of one's life, therefore, constantly grows larger, enlarging one's field of possibility. Ellison, who was named after Emerson and who has on several occasions confessed to a feeling of kinship with him, finally imagines his hero's life as the sort of liberating symbol that Emerson spoke of:

> The life of man is a self-evolving circle, which, from a ring imperceptibly small, rushes on all sides outward to new and larger circles, and that without end. The extent to which this generation of circles, wheel without wheel, will go, depends upon the force of truth of the individual soul.[22]

This, of course, is a classic vision of motion as endless possibility. Emerson, who argued that "the eye is the first circle," insisted that man may either be trapped or freed according to the power of his perception: "There are no fixtures to men if we appeal to consciousness."[23] In the same way, Ellison demonstrates in *Invisible Man* that his protagonist may inhabit such a dynamic world of unlimited becoming if he is able to *see* himself, his roots, and his environment in their essential terms. His claim that "the end was in the beginning" (431), therefore, is not a cry of despair. Instead, it is proof that he has discovered the primal stuff of the self and is now undertaking the open-ended journey that is such an essential feature of the African American picaresque tradition.

Charles Johnson has recently observed that Ellison's *Invisible Man* "has become something of a modern Ur-text for black fiction" since it dramatized more fully than any previous black text "the perceptual flux of experience that characterizes the black world."[24] In a similar way, Keith Byerman has characterized *Invisible Man* as a "paradigmatic work" that "created literary space" for many outstanding black fictionists writing from the late 1960s to the present. Byerman argues convincingly that by envisioning African American reality as "a world of organic process in which repetition and change are the only constants."[25] Ellison freed writers like Alice Walker, Toni Morrison, Ishmael Reed, Charles Johnson, James Alan McPherson, and Clarence Major from any ideological constraints that would limit their ability to explore the full range, complexity, and possibility of African American experience.

Ellison's urban world, therefore, has become a richly provocative metaphor of the fluidity and creativity of black American experience in the second half of the twentieth century. Designed by an oppressive society as a ghetto but experienced by invisible man as a liberating frontier, Ellison's city indeed has provided a "way out of no way" that has inspired a whole generation of black American writers. Like Ellison, Alice Walker both operated within and boldly transformed the American picaresque tradition. Just as Ellison rejected traditional pastoral space in favor of urban space as the locus for the open journey, Walker found new ways of adapting American picaresque narratives. This task was doubly difficult for Walker, however, because she confronted artistic and personal constraints that assumed gender as well as racial characteristics. Growing up in the segregated South that imposed severe limitations upon her both as a woman and as a black person, she also confronted, as an American writer, a tradition of journey literature that almost reflexively imagined women as hopelessly restricted by place and unable to find access to the liberating spaces explored by male picaros. The next chapter of this study will examine how Walker, like Ellison, was finally able to make a way out of no way, using the picaresque mode in fresh ways to explore the experience of black women in a richly affirmative manner.

3

Alice Walker's *The Third Life of Grange Copeland:* Black Women and the Picaresque Tradition

there is no fixed place on earth for man or woman.
—Walker, *Revolutionary Petunias*

I believe in change: change personal, and change in society.
—Walker, *In Search of Our Mothers' Gardens*

Surveying the fiction written by African American women up to the end of the 1960s, one is struck by the nearly complete absence of open-journey narratives found in works like Douglass's *Narrative* and Ellison's *Invisible Man. Our Nig*, the first novel published by a black American woman, concludes with its central character wandering as an invalid from town to town in search of a bare subsistence living after her husband has abandoned her and their child for an irresponsible life at sea. Frado's "tours," far from empowering her with freedom and independence, put her at the mercy of the "sympathy" of people who occasionally help her in small ways but, more often than not, confront her with "many frowns."[1] Rather than being given a new life by her movements, Frado merely disappears into empty space.

Nella Larsen's *Quicksand*, published some sixty-nine years later, concludes in an equally bleak way, with its protagonist Helga Crane exhausted rather than renewed by her travels and eventually sinking into the "quicksand" of a male-dominated culture that victimizes her. After moving from a black college in rural Alabama to New York City and then to Copenhagen, Helga returns to the Deep South, to a "tiny Alabama town" that provides her with a "place" that she hopes will give her a stable and satisfying identity. But she marries a fundamentalist preacher who suffocates her with an

61

enslaving life that includes living in an "ugly brown house" redolent with the "odor of sweat . . . stale garments . . . [and] manure." Bearing five children in less than four years, she feels physically "used-up" and spiritually numbed by the "quagmire" and "bog" that her life has become. The novel concludes with her inwardly and outwardly paralyzed, overwhelmed by a sense of "suffocation" and "asphyxiation."[2]

Jesse Fauset's *Plum Bun*, a major work of the Harlem Renaissance, contrasts sharply with picaresque novels written by black male writers during this period. Unlike Claude McKay's *Home to Harlem* and Langston Hughes's *Not Without Laughter,* which end with their respective heroes moving individualistically to wide-open urban spaces that offer new possibilities, *Plum Bun* concludes with its central character Angela Murray eagerly awaiting her return home from Europe so that she can marry, reestablish her relationship with her sister, and thus begin to define herself in terms of the "stable fixtures of family life." Indeed, *Plum Bun* may be seen as a sustained reductio ad absurdum of the open picaresque novel. For most of the book Angela Murray behaves like a picaresque figure who feels "enchained" by her position as a black woman in American society and who travels widely through various places and social levels in search of "a larger, freer world." Very light-complexioned, she decides to pass for white, feeling that this will provide her with the physical and social mobility she mistakenly feels will make her happy. But she eventually discovers that this perverse kind of "open" journey will only lead her to a rootless, valueless life of purposeless drifting. She finally equates restless movement with a lack of identity and placement in a society held together with meaningful traditions as a necessary prerequisite for the establishment of selfhood:

> But the urge to wander was no longer in the ascendent. The prospect of Europe did not seem as alluring now as the prospect of New York had appeared when she lived in Philadelphia. It would be nice to stay put, rooted; to have friends, experiences, memories.

Rejecting movement through open space that promises her constant development as an individual but that results in an empty materialism and selfishness that blocks her growth, she inverts the values of the picaresque novel by defining herself terms of "friends, ties, home, family."[3]

For the most part, successful journeys by African American female characters tend to be closed-ended rather than open-ended, resulting in the heroine coming to rest in a place that gives her a stable identity. Novels like Frances Harper's *Iola Leroy*, published in 1892, and Paule Marshall's *Praisesong for the Widow*, published in 1983, are vivid examples of what

Robert Stepto has called "narratives of immersion" in which the central characters consciously seek to return to a place that provides group consciousness and communal identity. Contrasting such narratives of immersion with what he describes as "narratives of ascent" leading to individual mobility and independence, Stepto claims that

> the immersion narrative is fundamentally an expression of a ritualized journey into a symbolic South, in which the protagonist seeks those aspects of tribal literacy that ameliorate, if not obliterate, the conditions imposed by solitude. The conventional immersion narrative ends almost paradoxically, with the questing figure located in or near the narrative's most oppressive social structure but free in the sense that he has gained or regained sufficient tribal literacy to assume the mantle of an articulate kinsman. As the phrase "articulate kinsman" suggests, the hero or heroine of an immersion narrative must be willing to forsake highly individualized mobility in the narrative's least oppressive social structure for a posture of relative stasis in the most oppressive environment, a loss that is only occasionally assuaged by the newfound balms of group identity.[4]

Iola Leroy, the heroine of Harper's novel, gives up the "highly individualized mobility" that a life of passing for white would provide her in post–Civil War America in order to be an "articulate kinsman" occupying a posture of relative stasis" that will allow her to gain contact with her roots as a black person. She acquires an education as a white woman in a northern college but returns South at the end of the novel, marries a black doctor, and commits herself to building a "new community" through her work as a teacher of mothers and children who have been freed from slavery.

Iola Leroy, like *Plum Bun*, can be seen as the exact reverse of open-journey books such as Douglass's *Narrative* and Ellison's *Invisible Man*, because its central characters move centripetally to a stabilizing place instead of moving centrifugally away from place to limitless directions in open space. Preferring relatively secure identities centered around the concept of "home" and rejecting the "restless and unsettled" lives of travel in the North and Europe, Harper's main characters settle down rather than light out for new territories. Although *Iola Leroy* begins with most of its black characters scattering in many directions when the Civil War erupts, it concludes with nearly everyone returning to the South during the Reconstruction period to rebuild black family life and reclaim the land that is needed as a basis for a stable society. After her father's death midway through the novel results in her being separated from her mother and brother, Iola is finally reunited with both as they reconstitute their family. Furthermore, she establishes a "cosy home" in North Carolina with her husband and renews family bonds with her uncle and great aunt, who buy and restore a nearby plantation. Bringing this vision of societal and family "order" to a culmination is Uncle Daniel, a person of immense stability and a touchstone of traditional black values who has remained in the South during the Civil War and who finally occupies "a nice little green cabin" that makes him "snug as a bug in a rug." Uncle Daniel, who is described on the novel's final pages as "a welcome guest in every home," is the moral center of the universe imagined by *Iola Leroy*, a stable world centered in reconstructed place, recovered traditions, and restored family relationships.[5]

Although Alice Walker in a later book such as *The Color Purple* would find the pastoral, closed narrative attractive, for the majority of her career as a writer she has operated in the open-ended picaresque mode that is so important in African American literary tradition. In *In Search of Our Mothers' Gardens* she argued that as a black writer she has a powerful sense of participating in a dynamic tradition that associates human growth and liberation with open movement, a tradition that is not nearly as available to white fiction writers. Feeling that the mainstream of modern American fiction is enervated by a pessimism that causes white writers "to end their books and their characters' lives as if there were no better existence for which to struggle,"[6] she feels inspired by a much more hopeful and vital black picaresque tradition arising from the slave narratives. While "the gloom of defeat is thick" in most modern fiction produced by white American writers,

> By comparison, black writers seem always involved in a moral and/or physical struggle, the result of which is expected to be some kind of larger freedom. Perhaps this is because our literary tradition is based on the slave narratives, where escape for the body and freedom for the soul went together. . . . (5)

It is no surprise, therefore, that the black writer who most deeply influenced Walker was Zora Neale Hurston, whose imagination was fired by images of open movement. Becoming "hooked" on Hurston's fiction during her own formative years, Walker saw Hurston's work as a model, "a key to a storehouse of varied treasure" (12). In this sense, most of Walker's fiction can be seen as signifying in a celebratory way on Hurston's picaresque fictions. Like Hurston, Walker was deeply preoccupied throughout her career with the quest for human liberation through open motion. As the narrator of *Meridian* stresses,

> [B]lack women were always imitating Harriet Tubman—escaping to become something unheard of . . . black women struck out for the unknown. They left home scared and came back (some of them) successful secretaries and typists. . . .
>
> Then there were simply the good-time girls who came home full of bawdy stories of their exploits in the big city; one watched them seduce the local men with dazzling ease, some who used to be lovers and might be still. In their cheap, loud clothing, their newly repaired teeth, their flashy cars, their too-gold shimmering watches and pendants—they were still a success. They commanded attention. They deserved admiration. Only the rejects—not of men, but of experience, adventure—fell into the domestic morass that even the most intelligent white girls appeared to be destined for.[7]

Many of Walker's early stories, which were eventually published in *In Love and Trouble*, celebrate such an open journey of "experience, adventure" as a means of liberation from a "domestic morass," restrictive roles imposed by a society intent on oppressing women and blacks. Thus the opening story "Roselily" consciously juxtaposes two levels of action: (1) a marriage ceremony that will trap the central character in lifeless domestic routine, and (2) her inward thoughts about escape to the North and a freer, more independent life. As the stiff ceremony drones on, Roselily feels "yoked" and her body "itches to be free of satin and voile."[8] Her only relief comes from imagining "the silvery gray car" that will transport her by moving out of "the darkness of Mississippi" (9) into Chicago, where she hopes to find "a new life" (7). Whether or not she will find such a new life is open to debate, but this much is clear—Roselily has an instinctive fear of stasis, seeing it as a kind of death, and equates life with movement itself.

The narrator of "Really *Doesn't* Crime Pay?" makes a similar equation. Trapped in a barren marriage that reduces her to "holding a baby or going shopping" (15), she sees her new suburban house as an extension of her numbed personality. Looking out the windows of "this house with a thirty-year-old mortgage" (10), she thinks of the futility of her past life and the emptiness of her future. Her one moment of relief has been a brief affair with a young writer described as "a vagabond . . . from no solid place, going to none" (12). After she is betrayed by him, she is confined to a mental institution. The story ends, however, with her restored to health, intent on abandoning her husband and his house, desiring to "leave them forever without once looking back" (23).

Walker's second collection of stories, *You Can't Keep a Good Woman Down* also contains a number of women who liberate themselves through open movement. The central character in "The Lover" feels restricted by her roles as wife and mother and journeys from her conventional midwestern home to a New England writer's colony where she enjoys many new freedoms, including a lover. Although she does return home at the end of the story, her newly aroused restlessness inspires her to dream of more journeys "to all the faraway countries, daring adventures, passionate lovers still to be found."[9] Imami, the narrator of "The Abortion," is likewise dissatisfied by ordinary middle-class roles and feels that "Her aim had never been to marry but to take in lovers who could be sent home at dawn, freeing her to work and ramble" (73). She finally packs up and leaves her husband for a new set of possibilities elsewhere.

The book's concluding story "Source" contrasts two women in terms of their capacities for open motion and personal development. Anastasia has an intense suspicion of the flux of life, claiming, "I knew I had to merge this self with something elemental and stable or it would shatter and fly away" (167). Deeply afraid of change and becoming herself, she subordinates her identity to men, first of all Source, a self-styled guru who believes that "the universe is unchangeable" (153) and that she should therefore accept the role of one of his "slaves" (152). Eventually freeing herself of Source, she reenslaves herself by passing for white and marrying an Alaskan Indian, whom she sees as another "elemental" force who will resolve her identity crisis by imposing a fixed role on her. In fact, she will be smothered by this man just as she had earlier been stifled by Source. But Irene, the central character of the story, rejects Anastasia's fear of change, defining herself in protean terms. Her life is a series of restless moves through a great assortment of places including Arkansas, New York, Washington D.C., San Francisco, and Alaska. As she moves, she steadily grows, developing a new sense of independence and selfhood. By the end of the story she yearns for symbolic open space: "She long[s] for the sun" (135), a true "source" of life that will provide her with the limitless energy that her ever-changing self requires.

The Third Life of Grange Copeland offers an extremely complex view of the open journey. Central to the novel is a powerful thematic tension between her characters' strong desire for a stable life centering around a "home" and their equally potent inclinations toward radical change, the "new life" brought about by open journeying. These two powerful drives are merged in Brownfield's recurrent daydream in which he imagines himself as owning both a beautiful mansion and an elegant car:

> As he stroked his shoes carelessly with a rag, Brownfield sank into his favorite daydream. He saw himself grown-up, twenty-one or so, arriving at home at sunset in the snow. In his daydream there was always snow. He had seen snow only once, when he was seven and there had been a small flurry at Christmas, and it had made a cold, sharp impression on him. In his daydream snow fell to the earth like chicken feathers dumped out of a tick, and gave the feeling of walking through a quiet wall of weightlessness and suspended raindrops, clear and cold on the eyelids and the nose. In his daydream he pulled up to his house, a stately mansion with cherry-red brick chimneys and matching brick porch and steps, in a long chauffeur-driven car. The chauffeur glided out of the car first and opened the back door, where Brownfield sat puffing on a cigar . . . Brownfield's wife and children—two children, a girl and a boy—waited anxiously for him just inside the door in the foyer. They jumped all over him showering him with kisses. While he told his wife of the big deals he'd pushed through that day she fixed him a mint julep.[10]

Sensing that he lives in a cold, white world of "snow" that can freeze him, Brownfield takes refuge in a warm family life and his "luxuriously warm limousine" (19). In reality, however, he and all of the novel's other characters must confront a cold "white" world without the benefit of stable families or exotic cars that can whisk them off to other places. In this novel the South is a place of terrible entrapment that destroys family life and enslaves blacks to an endless cycle of physical and spiritual poverty. Grange's role as a sharecropper turns him into "stone or a robot" (8) and imposes complete "submission" (5) on his wife Margaret. Their son Brownfield, whose entire life is a frightening extension of southern values and who comes to develop a perverse love of the South while in prison, lives in a condition of nearly total paralysis. Sharecropping threatens him with "the shadow of eternal bondage" (49) and his marriage soon becomes "another link in the chain that held him to the land" (50). Although he shows some signs as a young man of freeing himself by attempting to move out of the South, "his dreams of the North died early" (55) and he is content to accept his place in southern society—"he fitted himself to the slot in which he found himself" (59). This extreme passivity gradually erodes his spirit until he becomes a pathological figure intent on destroying his wife and children when they display any signs of rejecting the static roles that southern society impose on them. He always interprets their drive for movement and freedom as an indictment of his own depleted life.

Given such a numbing, paralyzing world, several characters attempt to save themselves by undertaking various kinds of journeys. Josie's daughter Lorene lights out to the North and is never heard from again. Grange, whose imagination has been fired by his brother-in-law Silas's exploits in New York, leaves the sharecropping work that has "stupefied" (12) him and simply takes off: "He had not even comprehended what he was running to. He was simply moving on to where people said it was better" (140). However, like Silas, who ends up a drug addict killed in a liquor store robbery, Grange eventually discovers that the North as a real place is a cruel hoax. Although he goes there to pursue his dream of "living free" (144), he is reduced to a condition of "solitary confinement" (145). Ironically, his experiences in New York are a depressing repetition of his existence in the South because all aspects of life in both places are rigidly controlled by whites: "He found that wherever he went whites were in control; they ruled New York as they did Georgia; Harlem as they did Poontange Street" (140).

Brownfield's abortive journey North is also doomed because it too results in his repeating the failures of the life he has always known in the South. After his mother dies, he rejects the offer to continue on Shipley's farm as a sharecropper and heads north in pursuit of "his own freedom" (24). But his journey soon gets stalled when he arrives at the Dew Drop Inn, where he becomes seduced by Josie, his father's former mistress. From this point on, he begins to realize that "his own life was becoming a repetition of his father's" (54). For the rest of the novel he becomes entrapped by his father's "first" life, an existence of grinding poverty and marital infidelity that robs him of the ability to live a fruitful life. Like his father, he leaves Josie to marry a more respectable woman, whom he comes to resent and then makes into a "submissive, accepting wife" (55) who cannot threaten his damaged ego. He also attempts, like Grange, to further repair his male ego by making Josie his mistress and inspiring terror in his children, whom he beats mercilessly. By the end of the novel he attempts to reenslave his daughter Ruth by taking her away from Grange, and this perverse desire morally paralyzes him, destroying what is left of his humanity:

> But as he lay thrashing about, knowing the rigidity of his belief in misery, knowing he could never change or renew himself, for his changelessness was now all he had, he could not clarify what was the duty of love; whether to prepare for the best of life, or for the worst. Instinctively, with his own

life as an example, he had denied the possibility of a better life for his children. He had enslaved his own family, given them weakness when they needed strength, made them powerless before any enemy that stood beyond him. Now when they thought of "the enemy," their own father would straddle their vision. (227)

Despite these failed journeys, the novel is saved from nihilistic despair by the fact that it is centered in two other interrelated journeys that endow it with richly affirmative meanings. The first is Grange's return to Georgia, where he begins his "third" life after growing embittered about his "second" life in Harlem. This journey produces a dramatic change in his character. Ruth had lost her parents when Brownfield murdered Mem, and Grange becomes a loving surrogate father for her. Unlike Brownfield who tries to weaken his children, Grange strengthens Ruth by providing her with an emotionally secure "home" on the farm that he and Josie buy with the money they get from the sale of the Dew Drop Inn. Ruth therefore avoids the problem that has made it difficult for Brownfield to move in a humanly meaningful way. His impotent drifting is explained by the fact that he has never had an adequate foundation in life:

> He was expected to raise himself up on air, which was all that was left after his work for others. . . . He was never able to do more than exist on air; he was never able to build on it. . . . (54)

Ruth, however, can move steadily toward a liberating new life because she has been brought up on much more than "air"—Grange's nurturing has provided her with the emotional and spiritual base she needs to develop a resilient self that is capable of undertaking the open journey so often celebrated in classic American and Afro-American literature. For she can indeed "build on" the three lives that Grange has lived as a way of moving toward her own protean identity containing unlimited "lives."

Grange's farm, therefore, should not be seen as a definite *place* that imposes fixed identities on people but rather as a pastoral space, a symbolic world of indeterminate possibilities. It is important to realize that Walker does not establish the farm as a romantic setting suggesting her love of southern "place." Surely Grange never evinces any love for Georgia in particular or for the South in general—"he hated it as much as any place" (141). He returns to Baker County because he is interested in creating a "home" (141) by transforming a restrictive place into liberating "space." When he fences off his property from the surrounding area he can make it a "sanctuary" (155), a "refuge" (156) distinct from southern society where he can be free and independent, a "reborn man" (157). His journey back to a pastoral world he creates is then a quest for the same sort of life-giving space that the Puritans sought in a New World "sanctuary" or Frederick Douglass sought by heading to the North.

It is important to realize also that Ruth must eventually leave this pastoral world to realize her own identity. Space, unlike place, can not be passively inherited but must be actively created by the traveler. Although Ruth as a young girl is nurtured by the home with which Grange provides her, she must, like most American heroic figures, finally break away from her home in order to undertake her own life's journey. For she comes to realize that her options in the world she was given are extremely limited—not only will the white world reduce her to a maid or a schoolteacher but the black community, which is sharply critical of her life with Grange, restricts her to the status of a pariah. When she asks Grange "What *am* I going to do when I get grown?" he tells her that she can stay on their farm "till kingdom come" (193). But she immediately rejects such a static conception of her future, telling him "I'm not going to be a hermit" (193). The same fences that give him a sense of security eventually induce claustrophobia in her. She needs unlimited space if she is to fulfill the deepest promptings of her ever-growing self.

The final quarter of the novel, therefore, dramatizes her plans for leaving home so that she can "rise up" (196) on her own. Her dreams of freedom first take the form of going North and she clearly tells Grange "I want to get away from here someday . . . I think I'll go North like you did" (193). Later she thinks vaguely of going to Africa and by the end of the novel she is deeply stirred by the prospect of becoming part of the Civil Rights movement. The exact direction she will pursue is never made precisely clear nor could it be. Like most American heroes, she has a lucid notion of the places she must leave but keeps an indeterminate vision of the space to which she will move. And like the Jews in Exodus, she must leave an all too real "Egypt" in order to experience a mythical "promised land." Grange delights in telling her the story of Exodus "for perhaps the hundredth time" (209) because he wants to strengthen her imagination for flight, so that she can avoid the "numbness" (210) that has blighted so much of his own life.

Although Walker is deliberately vague about the end point of Ruth's journey in order to stress its open, indeterminate quality, she emphatically points out that it will be radically different from the failed journeys undertaken by several other characters. Unlike her sisters Daphne and Ornette who drift north, one to end up in a "crazy house" (218) and the other to end up in a whorehouse, Ruth's movements will be intelligently directed by the sense of "mission" that Grange has given her to perform "some great and Herculean task" (198). Her active mind may be "always in flight" but it is endowed with purpose because it is always moving "toward something" (226), the creation of a protean self. Unlike Brownfield, whose life becomes a circle of failure because he is content to relive his father's "first" life, Ruth consciously rejects her father and everything he represents. Indeed, just at the moment when she tells him "I'm not yours," her consciousness is described as "a great dam about to fly open in her" (219). She will not be caught up, as was her mother, in the "close dungeon of his soul" (219) because she will not subordinate her fluid, dynamic consciousness to his monomaniacally rigid mind. Moreover, Grange's presence will help to support her but it will not stifle her, because he wants her to have much more than the three lives allotted to him. Telling her that his own life was restricted by the fact that "The world wasn't as big as it is now" (212), he encourages her to go to school and leave Baker County. He delights in spending evenings "examining maps, wondering about the places in the world he would never see" (214), all the while savoring the fact that Ruth will have the space that was inaccessible to him.

Ruth can enter the open spaces that will allow her to develop her identity because she finally learns what very few people in her world are aware of—that the self and society are not static givens, changeless absolutes, but a set of open possibilities for which she must take full responsibility. She observes Grange transform himself from a psychologically numbed person to one who can freely sacrifice his own life to ensure her growth. Although he has been *given* one life that will chain him to poverty and self-hatred, he *creates* through his own journeys two new selves that finally endow his life with human value. Central to Ruth's own development is her awareness that Grange's extraordinary growth is explained by his ability to take responsibility for his own life. Ultimately realizing that to categorically blame white society for all of his problems is truly to become a prisoner of the white world because such determinism denies him his free will, he declares to Brownfield "Nobody's as powerful as we make them out to be. We got our own *souls*, don't we?" (207). He creates a human self in his third life by reclaiming the free will he needs to move forward in life and thus break the cycle of futility that society has designed for him. As he tells his son, "We *guilty*, Brownfield, and neither one of us is going to move a step in the right direction until we admit it" (209).

Brownfield, unfortunately, cannot understand this critically important idea and so he remains until the end a pawn of Judge Harry and the racist

society he represents. But Ruth can liberate herself from the contaminations of the social world into which she was born when she realizes that she
is empowered to create her own self by moving in her own ways. Like
Richard Wright, who was forced to steal books from a Memphis library to
liberate his own mind and thus create new space in which to move, Ruth
eagerly reads the books Grange steals for her from the local library. Books
by "any romantic writer" (197), books about Africa, and books containing
"maps of the continents" (193) help to stir her spirit and free her will to the
point where she can map her life as she wishes. By the end of the novel she
sees life in dynamic terms as a "moving school" (231) that teaches her that
all things move and develop; nothing need be finally closed and static.

Even American society. A crucial phase of Ruth's development is her
growing awareness of society as a dynamic process instead of a static hier-
archy where everyone must fit into his or her "place." Observing the nightly
news, she becomes fascinated by "pictures of students marching" (232) as
they work for a more open and fluid society. Even in the Georgia backwa-
ter in which she has been raised there is dramatic evidence of meaningful
change—voter registration campaigns, interracial marriage, and the beginnings of integration. By the end of the novel, Ruth has been deeply stirred
by the "Movement" (237), which she feels will transform her world. As
she tells Grange in an important conversation late in the novel,

> "I think I believe like the students. . . . Ain't nothing wrong with *trying* to
> change crackers.
>   "What I want is somebody to change folks like your daddy, and some-
> one to thaw the numbness in *me*." He looked at his granddaughter and
> smiled.
>   "Course," he said, "you done thawed me some." (233)

Although people like Brownfield and Judge Harry are hopeless cases because their rigid minds have been frozen by the feudal society in which
they live, many people and social institutions are beginning to "thaw" at
the end of the novel. Dynamic forces are at work dissolving the stereotypes
that have crippled people in the past, creating new possibilities for people
like Ruth. Although Walker, whose life was profoundly transformed by her
participation in the Civil Rights movement,[11] does not provide us with a
naively romantic view of personal and political growth, she does believe
that vast changes will occur if people have the courage and imagination to
move toward these changes. The novel's somber ending, which depicts the
violence triggered by a failure of justice in a white-controlled system, reminds us that Ruth and her contemporaries are a long way from the fluid,

open society that they seek. But Walker stresses that they are at last moving in the right direction and this is no small cause for hope. Like the author's own mother, to whom she dedicates the novel, Ruth can triumph where others have failed because she "made a way out of no way."

Walker, in *In Search of Our Mothers' Gardens*, has observed that her sense of herself as "a socially conscious southern writer" has given her a complex "double vision" of her experience. This split vision prompts her both to celebrate certain aspects of southern life and also to criticize the severe racism that has been an integral part of southern culture:

> For not only is [the black southern writer] in a position to see his own world and its close community ("Homecomings" on First Sundays, barbecues to raise money to send to Africa—one of the smaller ironies—the simplicity and eerie calm of a black funeral, where the beloved one is buried way in the middle of a wood with nothing to mark the spot but perhaps a wooden cross already coming apart), but also he is capable of knowing, with remarkably silent accuracy, the people who make up the larger world that surrounds and suppresses his own.[12]

The Color Purple expresses one side of this complicated double vision, Walker's desire to achieve personal wholeness by reclaiming a sense of southern place and community. By the end of that novel Celie and Nettie regain the land from which their people were dispossessed and they attempt to unify their family with a Fourth of July celebration at which, in Celie's words, "We can spend the day celebrating each other."[13] All of the novel's main characters thus come to rest in a stable place that seems to offer them a secure "home." But as Trudier Harris has pointed out, this elaborate celebration of place is never believably dramatized in the novel, because it degenerates into sentimentality:

> From its opening in that paradoxical, nightmarish, fairy-tale vein, the novel moves through improbable events to the traditional passing out of presents in that contrived "happily ever after" ending. All the good guys win and the bad guys are dead or converted to womanist philosophy.[14]

Harris rejects the book's ending because she rightly believes that "In true fairy-tale fashion, it affirms passivity."[15] By romantically suggesting that Celie's and Nettie's unlikely recovery of a homeland will complete their

identities, the novel implies that the struggle is over and the characters
have dramatically achieved lasting happiness. But such an improbable ending is sharply at variance with the stark facts of southern life that Walker
has so effectively documented earlier in the book and throughout all her
previous writing.

The Third Life of Grange Copeland is centered in the other part of
Walker's double vision: her penetrating awareness of the racist society that
surrounds black life in the South and her reflexive desire to escape from
that world. This novel, far from being sentimental, brilliantly succeeds as a
work of art because it dramatizes its vision in a concrete and compelling
way. Ruth will indeed pay a substantial price for her restless journeys because she will never be able to achieve the security and wholeness of self
possible in a healthy society. But she is tough-minded enough to realize
that the southern society she leaves is anything but healthy and will only
trap her and poison the black life around her. In a world of severely limited
options, therefore, she correctly chooses movement over status and open
space instead of restrictive place because she knows it is her only way of
making a "way" out of "no way." Committing herself passionately to the
ever-changing real world with all its difficulties and costs, she nevertheless
discovers rich possibilities for growth that will never completely satisfy
her but will make available to her the same liberation that has been experienced by countless other heroic figures in American and African American
literature.

4

Toni Morrison's *Song of Solomon:*
Dialectics of Place and Space

I'm just a poor wayfaring stranger
A-travelling through this world of woe . . .
. . . I'm going over Jordan
I'm going home.
　　　　　　　　　—Traditional spiritual

And so when I couldn't stand it no more, I lit out.
　　　　　　　　　—*Adventures of Huckleberry Finn*

Throughout her entire career as a writer Toni Morrison has thought deeply about the relationships between place and space in the development of human identity. Her characters are typically offered two options for development. Although many of her key figures identify themselves in terms of the fixed values of a community life rooted in history and tradition, just as many of her central characters aggressively pursue lives of open motion that free them from the restrictions of the past and give them new conceptions of self. Such "undocumented" people are characterized by

> an inability to stay anywhere for long. Some were Huck Finns, some Nigger Jims. Others were Calibans, Staggerlees, and John Henrys. Anarchic, wandering they read about their hometowns in the pages of out-of-town newspapers.[1]

Thus *Sula* contrasts Nel Wright, who accepts a definite role in a settled community, with Sula Peace, someone who rejects any rigid notions of selfhood and views herself in radically open terms. Whereas Nel gladly accepts being "pinned to a tiny life" and claims that "Hell is Change,"[2]

75

Sula aggressively pursues restless movement in a fast-paced world outside the small town in which she was born. Like Huck Finn and many other American picaresque heroes, she feels that "doing anything forever and ever was hell" (108). In the same way, *Tarbaby* contrasts restless people moving through indefinite space with characters who prefer fixed identities provided by stable social groups. The novel ends, significantly, with Jadine Childs in open motion, rejecting any pressures that would limit her protean identity, while Son searches for the traditional society that he hopes will endow his life with continuity and permanence.

Morrison's more recent novels also dramatically contrast picaresque questers with settled people who position themselves in secure places. In *Beloved* Sethe sees herself as an extension of domestic space, declaring, "Whatever is going on outside my door ain't for me. The world is in this room." At one point in the novel she literally equates herself with her house, insisting that "This the place I am." Paul, on the other hand, envisions himself as a result of constant movement through indeterminate space. In the racist world of the post–Civil War South, which is intent on fixing him in a "place" of inferiority and dependence, his strategy for establishing an autonomous self is to "Move. Walk. Run. Hide. Steal and move on."[3] *Jazz*, likewise, contains restless people like Joe Trace, who cannot stand the "quiet" (49) life, with deeply rooted people like Henry Lestory, who resists with equal intensity the ceaseless flux and noise of modern life. While Joe's protean self rejects the static world of the rural South and delights in the constant change and movement of the urban North, Henry stays rooted in the rural South where he was born and raised. Even when whites during the Reconstruction attempt to violently force blacks out of Vesper County, Virginia, Henry resolutely stands his ground:

> Hunter refused to leave, he was more in the woods than in his cabin anyway, and seemed to look forward to spending his last days in the places he felt most comfortable. So he didn't haul his gear to a wagon. Or walk the road to Bear, then Crossland, then Goshen, then Palestine, looking for a work-place as Joe . . . did.[4]

Song of Solomon, one of Morrison's richest novels, grows out of this dialectic between the possibilities of space and the securities of place. What is unique about the book is its refusal to simplistically resolve the matter. Space and place are options for her characters, some of whom use these options well and others of whom use them poorly. Open motion, what Morrison often terms "soaring" and "flying," can destroy as well as liberate. In the same way, an attachment to a community rooted in time and place can either be a trap or a stabilizing force. No one's search for identity is wholly successful. What the novel presents instead is a tough-minded and dynamic interplay of ideas that never come to rest in any simple resolution. As a work in the American and African American picaresque traditions, therefore, *Song of Solomon* provides a thematic complexity and depth not often found in modern picaresque fiction. Refusing to naively celebrate the myth of open motion, as does Kerouac's *On the Road,* it nevertheless does not categorically negate the myth, as does Barth's *The End of the Road.* Morrison's road to human identity is still open, but it can be traveled only by those who are totally aware of the blueslike paradoxes and complexities of modern experience.

One of the most revealing indices of this complexity is the book's elaborate use of setting. Much of the action takes place in an unnamed town in Upper Michigan that borders Lake Superior. The setting is therefore both fluid and fixed, simultaneously inviting its inhabitants to settle down and to seek escape in radically open motion:

> Truly landlocked people know they are. Know the occasional Bitter Creek or Powder River that runs through Wyoming; that the large tidy Salt Lake of Utah is all they have of the sea and that they must content themselves with *bank, shore,* and *beach* because they cannot claim a coast. And having none, seldom dream of flight. But the people living in the Great Lakes region are confused by their place at the country's edge—an edge that is a border but not a coast. They seem to be able to live a long time believing as coastal people do, that they are at the frontier where final exit and total escape are the only journeys left. But those five Great Lakes which the St. Lawrence feeds with memories of the sea are themselves landlocked in spite of the wandering river that connects them to the Atlantic. Once the people of the lake region discover this, the longing to leave becomes acute, and a break from the area, therefore, is necessarily dream-bitten, but necessary nonetheless. It might be an appetite for other streets, other slants of light. Or a yearning to be surrounded by strangers. It may even be a wish to hear the solid click of a door closing behind their backs.[5]

This paradoxical doubleness is associated with the Great Lakes region throughout the novel. At once a traditionally American "frontier" offering renewal through motion, it is also an enclosure imposing harsh physical and moral restrictions on people. It does indeed provide the "final exit" of death, as we see in the first scene where Robert Smith commits suicide, but it also promises "new life," as is suggested when Macon Dead III's birth is triggered by the great excitement caused by Smith's fall. Such a world then is not, like the Great Salt Lake of Utah, "truly landlocked," because it is connected by way of the St. Lawrence River to the "sea," a symbolic area of indeterminate possibility.

Throughout the second half of the novel Morrison uses this nearly Whitmanesque sense of the sea as an open, fluid world. When Guitar urges Milkman to live his life more fully, the narrator tells us that "the clarion call in Guitar's voice filled his mouth with salt. The same salt that lay at the bottom of the sea . . . a taste so powerful and necessary that stallions galloped miles and days for 'it'" (84). The pungent, gingery smell of the lake, which it gets from its connection with the ocean, inspires the dreams of many characters, for "it smelled the way freedom smelled" (186). And when Milkman late in the novel is on the verge of a spiritual conversion, he cries out to Sweet: "I'm dirty and I want water . . . I need the sea" (330).

Ironically, though, no characters finally live their lives in terms of what the sea represents. Although Milkman ultimately feels "the whole complex deep blue sea" (330), he never reaches the ocean and only gets to bathe in a river that contains both relief and water moccasins. His mother and sisters remain "landlocked" all of their lives, confined for the most part by the physical restrictions imposed upon them by Macon Dead. And Macon, after wandering for a time as a young man, steadfastly refuses to leave the sterile Michigan town that is an exact correlative to his stagnant spirit. Some of Pilate's happiest days, however, are spent working on an island off the coast of Virginia, where she experiences a genuine community life and gives birth to her only child, Reba. But, driven on by her restlessness, she leaves the island to take up a life of inland travel for twenty years. Although "no place was like the island ever again" (148), she never returns there and finally takes up residence in the same confining town that her brother has settled in.

The town itself is also portrayed paradoxically. It is both a definite location whose mores and customs restrict its inhabitants and also a condition of placelessness where people are set floating in a bizarre world with only vague coordinates in space and time. It is never named and its chief landmarks are a series of oxymoronic inversions. Milkman is born in No Mercy Hospital and lives on No Doctor Street. Some physical descriptions provided in the novel are deliberately misleading. The town's main streets, Routes 6 and 7, are described as "leading to Pennsylvania" (4), falsely suggesting that the town is located in a state bordering Pennsylvania. Indeed, there is very little indication of the exact state in which the town is located until roughly halfway through the book, when the narrator describes Milkman observing the state seal of Michigan in a train station. Therefore, when Guitar says to Milkman that "you don't live nowhere" (103), he is right in two ways. In a sense, Milkman is a misnamed, unplaced person who must move away from his Kafkaesque hometown to find out who he really is. But, as Guitar's double negative inadvertently makes clear to the reader, Milkman does not live "nowhere" but is instead tied to a small American town that, like e. e. cummings's "howtown," affixes an all too definite set of roles upon him.

Purposeful movement in such a world is usually problematic and sometimes impossible. Many characters are overwhelmed by the strange geography they inhabit and remain immobilized for most of their lives. Dr. Foster is literally "paralyzed" (12) by the drugs he uses in a futile attempt to escape the emptiness of his life. Except for a brief interlude at college, his daughter Ruth remains in the house on No Doctor Street that is "more prison than palace" (19). Macon Dead II, after a period of wandering brought on by the murder of his father, settles into the town and never leaves it. Everything about his life is profoundly static, from his car, which is described as a "hearse" (32), to his mind, which is characterized by its "numbness" (30). Hagar's "anaconda love" (137) threatens to paralyze Milkman and he breaks off from her in an attempt to avoid his parents' fate. Even Guitar, who early in the novel is associated with a bluesy wanderlust, is finally identified with a racist paranoia that freezes his mind and spirit. Randomly killing whites after any blacks have been murdered, "so the numbers can remain static" (159), he is just as mad as Empire State, a person who has been numbed by traumatic experiences.

It is not surprising, therefore, that most of the scenes that portray character growth deal with various kinds of open motion. Macon Dead I begins a new life by leaving the South after the Civil War and taking an epic journey North. Although he intends to go to a particular place, Boston, his inability to read signs lands him in Pennsylvania, where for twelve years he develops a farm, Lincoln's Heaven. Although he is eventually dispossessed of this land, Macon experiences a genuine conversion in the North. Lincoln's End is the only fully satisfying place in the novel, an Eden of love and plenty that is lost when whites murder for the land.

Throughout the novel such open movement is associated with expanded possibilities and deepened awareness. After striking his father in chapter 3, an act that brings his early life to a sudden halt, Milkman takes a long walk at night in search of Guitar. While walking alone he awakens to a number of truths previously hidden from him. The scene ends with his deciding to break away from his restrictive family past and to pursue a freer, more independent life. His train ride with his mother in chapter 5 is likewise an awakening experience that deepens his awareness of the past and opens his mind to the future. It results in his journey South toward a new definition of himself. His sister Corinthians also breaks out of the sterile routines of her life in an important motion scene when she meets Porter on a bus ride, an event that completely changes their lives. Their love saves her from utter stagnation and saves him from his monomaniacal commitment to the Seven Days, a group of fanatics rigidly devoted to acts of racial revenge. Significantly, their relationship is symbolized by his automobile, which provides them privacy and escape.

Moreover, the novel's two most important narrative sequences are Pilate's wanderings, described midway through the novel, and Milkman's journey south, which comprises the second half of the book. Both are "open" in two important ways: they are not consciously directed toward a particular place; and each is a process of self-discovery in which restrictive identities are dissolved and more fluid selves emerge.

Pilate's entire life is solidly in the tradition of American picaresque figures. An orphan who is literally without a navel, she "borned herself" (246). Like Natty Bumppo and Ishmael, she is a self-generating person whose wide travels give her a protean identity. The core of her life consists of twenty years of wandering during which she is almost entirely cut off from "a reliable source of human nourishment" (28). These free movements enliven rather than deaden her humanity, for they give her a liminal status that allows her contact with human society but also provide the distance necessary for her to stay clear of its contaminations. Her mind, which has "traveled crooked streets and aimless goat paths" 149), develops well beyond the stagnant thinking that limits most of the novel's other characters. Her mystical awareness, what the narrator calls her "peace . . . energy and singing" (304), stands in vivid contrast to Guitar's madness, Ruth's shallowness, and Macon's sterile pragmatism. For this reason, she is able to escape all the narrow roles that trap everyone else in the book. Resisting the demeaning jobs allowed most blacks because "she wanted to keep moving" (145), she avoids the empty work routines that enervate people like Robert Smith and Corinthians. Refusing to marry the man who gets her pregnant, she avoids the deadly marriage that suffocates Milkman's parents. But she also escapes the loveless isolation that psychologically stunts Guitar's growth. Although unmarried and outside the direct flow of human society, she is responsible for most of the acts of genuine love that the novel records—grieving for her father, protecting Milkman, and offering Ruth friendship. Her "alien's compassion for troubled people" (150) makes her the novel's richest characterization. Song of Solomon, like Huck-

leberry Finn, rests on the startling irony that only an outsider is able to feel and act upon the compassion that should be at the center of human society.

Milkman's entire story can be divided into two opposite phases: his life up to age thirty, which is portrayed as a series of false starts and dead ends; and his subsequent travels, which offer the possibility of transfiguration into a new life. Part 1, which concludes with his literally slamming the door on his own life, reduces most of his experiences to what his proper name suggests: activities that "make him dead." An unwanted child whom his father tried to abort, he grows up in a static household that separates him from normal forms of growth. His mother nurses him for an unnaturally long period because she wants to keep him in a state of dependency. Guitar initially liberates him from this trap by bringing him at age twelve to Pilate's house, where he "feels happy for the first time in his life" (17). His relationships with the widely traveled Pilate and Hagar give him access to avenues of development denied his sister and his parents. Eventually, however, he senses a need to grow beyond all the limits of the town. He feels trapped by the incestuous affair with his cousin Hagar when she begins to expect marriage, something he is deeply suspicious of. And his close friendship with Guitar deteriorates when it settles into a "groove" (120) and becomes "a one-way street" (154). Although Guitar tells him that if he wants to "fly" he had better "give up the shit that weighs [him] down" (180), he himself is filled with racial obsessions and dreams of "stationary things" (180), money, and power.

As the people around Milkman attempt to coerce him with their rigid expectations, he feels a reflexive desire to simply "light out." His trip to the South, although on one level motivated by an intent to find gold, is spurred on a deeper level by resolve to live in a newer, more fluid world:

> Milkman fantasized too, but not for the stationary things Guitar described.
> Milkman wanted boats, cars, airplanes, and the command of a large crew.
> He would be whimsical, generous, mysterious with the money. (180)

Whereas dreams of gold congeal Guitar's imagination by adding to his obsessions for materialism and racial retaliation, they help Milkman to envision expanded possibilities, a richer and freer human life. For these reasons, he is not altogether disappointed when he discovers in Danville that the gold is an illusion. Now he is free to pursue the original purpose of his journey, to simply "get away" (163)—an open quest toward the unknown.

Unfortunately, he makes the crucial mistake of informing Guitar about the purpose of his trip before leaving Michigan and, as a result, is followed wherever he goes. The rest of the novel consists of Milkman's very American desires for a "solo" (222) trip to the world of Solomon, the "solo man" who flew away from a restrictive past, and Guitar's relentless pursuit of him with the old life. Guitar, who earlier in the novel has been associated with liberation, is now clearly identified with a crippling past. Milkman is essentially correct when he tells his friend, "You're getting to be just like my old man" (106). Both figures bring death wherever they go because their growth was arrested at an early age by witnessing the brutal deaths of their fathers. Their steel-trap minds, which force Milkman into fulfilling their narrow plans for him, are the real impediments to his growth.

Critical discussion of the final meaning of Milkman's journey varies widely. Dorothy Lee argues that he achieves transcendence by integrating himself with the values of his community and racial past:

> Initiated into a real black community, he abandons false pride and atones for his errors in suffering. Releasing egotism, he affirms birth into a new life. Toni Morrison seems to tell her readers that Milkman's flight may be duplicated by all who can abandon the frivolous weights that held them down and, in so doing, ride the air.[6]

Joyce Wegs also sees a positive meaning to Milkman's journey but argues that it consists of his final rejection of "flight" in favor of embracing the black traditions he discovers at Shalimar. She views his final leap toward Guitar as a gesture of redemptive love and brotherhood.[7] Leslie Harris, on the other hand, regards Guitar as "an extension of the very negations Milkman has practiced"[8] and concludes that his final attempts to define himself consist of his resolve to destroy Guitar. Susan Blake contends that Milkman's journey culminates in "a solitary leap into the void," a gesture that is "not communal but existential."[9] Although the novel itself extols the life-giving nature of communal values, Milkman ultimately fails to act satisfactorily in terms of them.

For all their divergence, each of these readings of Milkman's journey has one thing in common: a reductive tendency to oversimplify the densely paradoxical texture of the novel in favor of a neater, more manageable thesis. Although Harris claims that the book is finally "less ambivalent than it appears,"[10] precisely the opposite is the case—its meanings increase in complexity the more closely we examine them.

From the very outset Milkman's journey is tangled with ironies, para-doxes, and contradictions that greatly enrich its meanings. Although his quest is initially motivated by an understandable desire to get away from the madness and greed represented by Guitar and his father, he involves both people in his plans for escape. Curiously, he asks his father's advice about his future, and, when he accidentally mentions the gold supposedly stored in Pilate's house, he allows him to convert his quest for indepen-dence into a mad hunt directed by others. Worse, he makes Guitar an ac-complice in stealing the gold, even though he knows Guitar will carry a gun and kill anyone black or white who gets in his way. Milkman's search for "a new life," therefore, is from the outset undercut by strong overtones of death.

What Morrison suggests by these contradictions is the radically di-vided nature of Milkman's mind and the extreme difficulty of his situation. Although he is consciously driven by a desire for an open journey, he is pulled away from it by a subconscious attachment to a dead past from which he must liberate himself. His father and Guitar, the two mentors of his early life, can now be easily dismissed by a simple act of will. They are part of a past that weighs him down and, in order for him to "fly," he must assimilate and transcend that past by living through a painful set of experi-ences that will confront him with a number of important tests.

Part 2 of the novel always involves two levels of awareness—Milkman's limited consciousness as it moves through a journey that he never fully understands and the narrator's mind as it presents that journey from a highly sophisticated, ironic perspective. For example, chapter 10 begins with a synopsis of the story of Hansel and Gretel, who run into the house "where a woman older than death lived" (221). While Milkman naively enjoys the airplane ride to a similar place of death, he feels "away from real life . . . free" (229). The narrator fully understands what the character has no idea of—that his travels will be a dangerous encounter rather than a simple escape. Morrison uses these ironic juxtapositions repeatedly throughout Milkman's trip. After he discovers that the Danville cave contains neither gold nor anything else of value, he wants to be "Free" (260) of the compul-sions that have led him to the cave. Instead of simply giving up on this fool's errand, however, he immediately heads to Virginia, partly in search of gold, even though he fully realizes that "the fine reasons for wanting it didn't mean a thing" (260). Although he has deluded himself into thinking he is in open motion, the narrator reminds us that he is simply following in Pilate's "tracks" (261).

The final five chapters further develop such ironies. At the precise moment in the bobcat hunt when Milkman feels he completely understands Guitar and actually experiences "a sudden rush of affection" (282) for him, he is nearly strangled by his "friend." Although he develops a number of romantic ideas about Shalimar containing a past that will easily solve his identity problems, he almost gets killed there in a senseless brawl and perhaps dies there in the novel's first episode. As the narrator makes clear, the Deep South is not simply a primitivistic womb—although it surely does contain a usable past that must be grasped, it also contains a history that has "maimed" (282) many people. The jagged cut that Milkman receives in the general store fight links him ominously with Saul and Guitar, both of whom have been deeply scarred by their southern experiences The South therefore offers both the healing warmth of Sweet and the terrible violence of Saul.

The final two parts of Milkman's journey are surrounded by even sharper ironies. When he returns home in high excitement over his southern discoveries, he is knocked cold by Pilate just as he extends his arm to her in "warm embrace" (335). While he simplistically views his travels as the discovery of his new life, she regards them more realistically as the abandonment of her granddaughter, who died after he left her. The final pages of the novel, often cited as evidence for Milkman's achievement of selfhood are also filled with complicating ironies. Although Milkman intends to give Pilate the ultimate satisfaction of burying her father's bones in Virginia, the trip results in her being murdered after she is needlessly exposed to Guitar. The past that Milkman has so rapturously brought back to Michigan causes her death and perhaps his own demise as well. In the novel's final scene, he perhaps proves the aptness of his given name of Macon (Makin') Dead by foolishly offering his life to the psychopathic Guitar:

> "You want my life? . . . You need it? Here." Without wiping away the tears, taking a deep breath or even bending his knees—he leaped. As fleet and bright as a lodestar he wheeled toward Guitar and it did not matter which one of them gave up his ghost in the killing arms of his brother. For now he knew what Shalimar knew: If you surrendered to the air you could *ride* it. (341)

Although Milkman's mind is apparently filled with romantic notions about the meaning of his act, the narrator's broader, more incisive awareness allows us to view the scene in more realistic terms. Fighting Guitar is suicidal because he is armed and Milkman is not. And if Guitar is a "brother" it is only in the sense that Cain was Abel's brother. Milkman's act of "riding" in the air in the novel's final paragraph therefore should not be simply equated with the heroic soaring mentioned in the novel's inscription:

> The fathers may soar
> And the children may know their names

Whereas this kind of open motion provides black people with a heroic myth enabling them to better identify themselves, Milkman's actions take place on a realistic, not a mythic, level. His riding the air may be seen by some as an act of transcendence, but it is just as valid to see it as a repetition of the demented flying done by Robert Smith, the insurance agent who falls to his death in the novel's opening scene. The book's radically open ending, which artfully cuts off the action before it can be completed, makes it impossible to assign a definitive meaning to Milkman's narrative. But it is quite possible that he, like Robert Smith, has been finally trapped by circumstances beyond his control and makes a "final exit" from life in sheer desperation. To summarize, there are signs that Milkman's trip to the South has provided him with a new awareness that enables him to "fly" to a new identity, but these signs are countered by opposite evidence. His story, therefore, remains an open dialectic a set of ideas in motion rather than a neatly resolved narrative.

Embedded in such irreducible ambiguities, Milkman's life perhaps may be best imagined as a symbolic circle that yields two entirely opposite meanings. True to her richly ambivalent method, Morrison employs the circle in two strikingly different ways throughout the novel: as a deterministic trap and as a mystical sign of continuity and harmony. Ruth Foster's closed existence is epitomized by the watermark that mars her otherwise elegant dining room table; it is "a cloudy grey circle" (11), which she tries unsuccessfully to hide. And the hunters in chapter 11 circle the bobcat as they stalk and eventually kill it. But the circular dancing performed by the children of Shalimar as they sing the Song of Solomon provides very positive meanings, since it strongly suggests that their lives are a circle of continuity connected to a vital past. Morrison does not clearly indicate which of these radically opposed meanings are finally applied to Milkman's story as birds circle him and the dying Pilate in the final scene. The birds' motion, like most of the important movements of Milkman's life, are irreducibly ambiguous, suggestive of meanings too complex for simple formulation.

This is not to claim that *Song of Solomon* ultimately negates the myth of open motion so often celebrated in African American and American literatures. Although Milkman's movements are seen as a fascinatingly ironic blur and characters such as Corinthians do not achieve satisfying lives by settling down to conventional married lives, Pilate's life is always associated with various kinds of open movement. Whereas we never really know if Milkman's story is finally revealed by either his life-giving nickname or his deadly proper name, Pilate's narrative clearly is at odds with the grotesque biblical allusion attached to her name. Rather than condemning people to death, she remains faithful to those she loves, making heroic sacrifices for them that culminate in her own death. In fact, the grim name that is arbitrarily imposed on her at birth is subtly transfigured by the beauty of her life. She finally becomes a "pilot"—a person whose sensibilities allow her to move well beyond a social world that tries to suffocate her. She becomes a guide to others, trying to get them to likewise move in free, purposeful ways.

Paradoxically she is a person who "without ever leaving the ground . . . could fly" (340). This "flying" is carefully contrasted with that attempted by all other people in the novel. Mr. Smith dies because his pathetic artificial wings fail to sustain him as he jumps off the roof of No Mercy Hospital. But Pilate figuratively soars in the very same scene by singing the blues song in a "powerful contralto" (5) that lifts her beyond Smith's plight, elegiacally assimilating and transcending his pain. When Milkman discovered at age four that he could not fly, he "lost all interest in himself" (9). His "bereft" imagination renders his life "dull" (9) but Pilate's superior imagination allows her to respond to even the meanest experience with "peace . . . energy, singing" (304). Ruth Foster is like the peacocks that are so weighed down by their fine plumage that they can never truly fly, but Pilate is completely indifferent to the world's finery, endowed as she is with a spirit that can soar well beyond her outward circumstances. She even surpasses Solomon himself, who flew back to Africa away from an environment that tried to "yolk" and "choke" (307) him. While Solomon's flight resulted in his abandoning his friends, his wife, and his twenty children, Pilate's soaring spirit and physical restlessness never prevent her from caring for those she loves. Deeply believing that "You can't fly off and leave a body" (336), she lives a life of dynamic "equilibrium" (136) that combines the best features of the stabilities of place and the fluid possibilities of space. Emphatically contradicting the sentiments of a traditional blues song that claims that "when a woman gets the blues she runs to her room and cries, but when a man gets the blues he takes a train and rides," Pilate is one of the most remarkable picaresque figures in the American and African American literary tradition.

But Pilate's story does not resolve the thematic tensions of *Song of Solomon*. The open, dialectical nature of Morrison's novel prevents any single character from assuming a central role that would coerce the book into a single perspective that would reduce its thematic complexity to a single flat "meaning." Essentially polyvalent, *Song of Solomon* finally regards open movement and stable placement in fundamentally ambivalent ways. In an interview with Mel Watkins, Morrison stressed her split response to open movement:

> [B]lack men travel, they split, they get on trains, they walk, they move. I used to hear these old men talk about travelling—which is not getting from here to there, it's the process—they even named themselves after trains. It's a part of black life, a positive, majestic thing, but there is a price to pay—the price is the children. The fathers may soar, they may triumph, they may leave, but the children know who they are; they remember half in glory, half in accusation.[11]

Although part of Morrison endorses open movement as a "process" leading to expanded possibility and growth, another part of her points out that people can pay a steep "price" for such movement. Children, who have been deprived of whole and stable families by the "soaring" of their fathers, view such movement "half in glory, half in accusation," duplicating Morrison's ambivalence. But it must also be stressed that Morrison is equally split in her response to lives rooted in place and tradition. As all of her novels, and especially her most complex novel, *Song of Solomon,* reveal, such placement also has a very steep price, for it can cripple the human spirit.

Morrison, therefore, offers her readers a complex dialectic rather than a simple message. Her themes are in constant movement and are not stated in any flat or fixed way. Charles Johnson's *Faith and the Good Thing,* the subject of the chapter that follows, is built in a similar way, making the reading experience itself an open journey toward endlessly proliferating meanings rather than a closed journey culminating in a single view of life. In this sense, it closely resembles *Song of Solomon* in form.

5

Charles Johnson's *Faith and the Good Thing:* The Open Journey as Metaphysical Quest

It was a bitter thing to siphon your being from someone else.
—Johnson, *The Sorcerer's Apprentice*

But in terms of content, Charles Johnson's *Faith and the Good Thing* conceives of the African American open journey in ways that are quite different from the open journeys portrayed in either *Song of Solomon* or *The Third Life of Grange Copeland*. Whereas the journey depicted by Morrison is cultural in nature, portraying the hero's search for a new understanding of the history of his people, and whereas Walker's journey is largely personal in scope, envisioning the heroine's conscious separation from the segregated South to define herself in fresh terms, the journey portrayed in Johnson's novel is metaphysical in character. That is, it is centered in Faith Cross's quest for truth itself, "the good thing" that she imagines can be the guiding principle of her life. As the novel's first paragraph reminds us, such a truth is "hidden by the gods to torment mankind for sins long forgotten."[1] This kind of truth can be found only through arduous journeying, the heroine's quest to find a metaphysical basis for her identity.

Unlike classical metaphysical quests portrayed in books like Dante's *Commedia* and Bunyan's *The Pilgrim's Progress*, Faith's journey is strikingly antiteleological in character. Whereas the journeys undertaken by Dante's and Bunyan's heroes culminate in their arriving in a definite place that gives them a fixed identity grounded firmly in changeless absolutes, Faith feels confined by the very notion of place and must journey in uncharted space. Her open journey is a brilliant metaphor of how Johnson envisions the self as an endless process of becoming rather than as a static condition of being. Whenever Faith conceives of "the good thing" in static terms as a single absolute truth that can define her, she is stifled, but she is finally liberated by the notion that the object of her quest is truth that is dynamic, always evolving into new forms. For example, when her mother tells her "girl, get yourself a good thing" (4) she means that Faith should get married to a man who can provide her with material security and social status. When Faith does precisely this by marrying Isaac Maxwell, she finds herself numbed by a shallow, suffocating lifestyle that inhibits her growth and makes her one of the "dead living" (125). Likewise, when Rev. Brown asks her to center her life in a conventionally Christian notion of goodness, which he conceives as worshipping a changeless God who presides over a "shadowy cave fulla crazy sounds" (14), she rejects this because it does violence to her sense of the world as exciting, beautiful, and "good." She later tries to make Alpha Omega Holmes into her "good thing," but he also proves a disappointment, deserting her when she gets pregnant. As his name suggests, he too is a dead end, a "beginning" that soon turns into an "end" when circumstances challenge him to grow and he is unable to meet this challenge. Trapped by a static ideal of himself as "an eternal child" (157) who requires absolute freedom and independence, he is not able to transform himself so that he may embrace a new role as father, and he thus becomes anything but a "good thing" for Faith.

She ultimately realizes that the result of her quest cannot be a truth that other people define and impose on her but must be an always changing process that she must discover for herself. At the conclusion of the novel she understands that, through half truths and outright falsity, most of the people who have directed her life have given her false quests directed at static goals:

> Her body seemed already gone but her mind was clear, as transparent as bubbling spring water with shiny stones visible on the floor of the stream. Side by side at the stream's bottom were stones for the respective stances she'd endured: Lynch, Tippis, Lavidia, Brown, Maxwell, Barrett, and Big Todd. Their voices tramped through her mind with the force of a hunter's bootheel. . . . Not one of them knew of the Good Thing, or even believed in its possibility. . . . (183)

Truth is not the hard stones in the stream but the stream itself. Like Ellison's invisible man who ultimately comes to the conclusion that truth is not a static deposit but a dynamic flow, she finally realizes that there is no end to her quest and that she must immerse herself in the continuous flux of experience. Her life must therefore take the form of a journey that is as fluid as truth itself. As the Swamp Woman reminds her, "[T]here ain't no beginnin' and no end. . . . There ain't nothin' but searchin' and sufferin'"(189). Because "Dialectics don't hold no single truth" (189), Faith must always search for fresh truths that, like her, are always evolving, never standing still. Her quest, in other words, is an ongoing dialectical process rather than a teleological experience that can be neatly mapped in terms of a definite beginning, middle, and end. She must, like most African American picaros, leave the securities of place and move freely in various forms of uncharted space.

This is made clear at the beginning of the novel when she leaves her home after the death of her mother. Born into a traditional southern world where blacks are rigidly placed in a society that assigns very definite and changeless identities to all people, she finds it necessary to move toward new forms of space when she loses her mother, who, up to this point in her life, has been "the center of [her] world" (13). The familiar place that centered her early life dissolves when Faith returns home after the funeral to discover that she can no longer relate to such a place:

> The kitchen had changed. You could locate nothing misplaced, nothing out of the ordinary, for as a housekeeper Lavidia was meticulous; but the kitchen's former gloss of permanence was gone. Its smell was still that of the dry cotton fields just outside the open window above the sink, of browning bread Lavidia had baked just two nights before; yet Lavidia was gone. Though old, dissipated, sometimes evil, she had been the focus of the farmhouse since her husband's death, its most crucial node, surely its mistress. Without her the kitchen, the house, the world, just fell apart. (5)

Although surely painful at the time, such a dissolving of place helps to liberate Faith, for it is the first time in her life that she can see beyond the "gloss of permanence" in her life, looking through the windows of her mother's house to the ever-growing "fields." Faith is now prepared to move beyond the "wall against which Lavidia had measured her height across eighteen years" (6) and thus begin to measure her own growth in her own ways. Feeling that if she now touched this wall it might "tumble away" (6), she experiences an immediate sense of psychological growth—her thoughts race like "wild animals" (6) and she begins to envision new possibilities for herself that range well beyond her mother's experience. As the "walls receded from her, meeting at apexes a dizzy distance away" (6), Faith instinctively recoils from the place that has limited her growth and eagerly moves toward new space that will stimulate her growth.

This first takes the form of detaching herself from her parents' farmhouse, because "the cabin defined her memories" (16), and then lighting out indefinitely south until "her flight took her to the edge of the swamp" (16), an indeterminate space that both frightens and intrigues her. This liminal world puts her at the boundaries of the known and the unknown. Faith now feels a strong, instinctive need to break away from her restrictive past life; she steps into the boundless world of the unknown when she enters the Swamp Woman's shack. This new space frees her from the limits of the familiar world and gives her access to the miraculous and strange. More importantly, it gives her a new way of regarding "the good thing" that she now wants to make the object of her quest. Whereas her mother defined the good thing in very narrow, trivialized terms as marrying a man who would supply her with material comfort, status, and security, the Swamp Woman envisions her pursuit of the good thing in metaphysical terms:

> "I've thought a lot about the Good Thing" she said, counting off the possibilities on the twelve taloned fingers of her right hand, "and I figure it must be the right functionin' of an organism as it participates in a form, or the fulfillment of a teleological principle inherent in all matter, or gettin' in the right relationship with the Lord (or Lords, or y'self, dependin' upon your persuasion) . . . or a leap of faith, or abolishin' private property, or maybe avoidin' Bad Faith." The Swamp Woman giggled as though she'd told a joke. "Take your pick, sweetheart." (24)

Whereas Faith naively desires "the *one* Good Thing" (24) that will provide her with an absolute truth, the Swamp Woman challenges her with a more complex and liberating vision of truth because she sees truth as multiple, not single, and protean, not static. She therefore widens Faith's vision and begins her process of liberation by giving her an ongoing quest worth pursuing. For if the pursuit of the "Good Thing" as the Swamp Woman defines it in capital letters at first frightens and confuses Faith, it also liberates her from the trivialized "good thing" that her mother spelled in lowercase letters. This new goal promises to put an end to Faith's "bondage" (30), because it frees her from the limiting identities that others try to impose on her and sets her on the road to self-discovery.

Before meeting the Swamp Woman, Faith's life has consisted of various kinds of "bondage." On a personal level, she has been enslaved by her mother, who limits her growth by driving away her boyfriends and brainwashing her with fundamentalist religion. On a broader level, she is enslaved by southern society, which "places" blacks in demeaning roles and then severely punishes them for stepping out of these roles. Southern whites lynch Faith's father when he rebels against racist codes and also humiliates Faith when she is not allowed to use rest rooms at gas stations and is forced to relieve herself in the fields. Southern sharecropping keeps blacks at the bottom of society by robbing them of the fruits of their labors and putting them at the mercy of whites who control the system. The Swamp Woman therefore urges Faith to leave the South and "Go to Chicago" (27) in search of a better life. Chicago is a radically new space offering new possibilities not likely to be found in the constricted world of Hatten County, Georgia. While such a new space is at times terrifying and subjects Faith to considerable suffering, this pain results in a significant deepening of Faith's consciousness, which helps her to move more effectively on her quest.

To suggest that Chicago is more space than place, Johnson describes it in a very suggestive, impressionistic way rather than realistically reproducing it as the sort of fully reified setting found in naturalistic novels such as Dreiser's *Sister Carrie*. Faith's journey to Chicago is not directed toward any particular location in the city, since she has no clear idea of exactly where she will stay or where she can find "the good thing." When she steps off the train, she sees the city as a blur of apparently random motion and disconnected images that move too quickly for her to comprehend. She is disoriented by the "fast-moving crowd" (49) and the blare of car horns. Feeling "lost, directionless" amid such "chaos" (52), she soon falls victim to Barrett, who robs her, and Tippis, who rapes her.

Throughout the novel Chicago is portrayed as an indeterminate space, a dark mindscape revealing Faith's feelings and thoughts. After she is raped by Tippis, her mental desolation is revealed by the "cold, empty streets" (61) on which she walks. The "winding streets" that she later walks as a prostitute can be seen as the winding corridors of her darker, instinctual self into which she journeys as she becomes transformed by the city from a naive waif to a hardened streetwalker. Shortly before accepting Maxwell's proposal of marriage, she notices that "fog descended upon the city like a curse" (121), again reflecting her confusion as she gets lost in a sterile relationship that reduces her to the level of an automaton. When her marriage dissolves after Maxwell expels her from their apartment, the city again is presented as an eerie underworld reflecting her deepest feelings. Walking the streets alone, she thinks "Chicago seemed darker than she could ever recall seeing it" (174).

Midway through the novel Faith experiences a psychological crisis after disrupting a meeting at the Church of Continual Light. She walks through the streets, which she regards as a symbol of modern anarchy, a world disintegrating into purposeless motion,

Thinking: *this* is home—a strangely ordered city seething beneath its veneer of rigidity and regulation with growing pockets of anarchy, theft, murder, a death every day, and crimes which the authorities suppressed quickly, like a finger dousing a candle's flame. All night the city lamps were lit, all night the borders of order buckled and receded and were restored before day. A losing battle. The truth would steal into this and every city like a Mongol horde, turning dreams into nightmares, incrusting even the most brilliant, self-certain careers with the dust and decay of time. (80)

Chicago at this point in the novel becomes a terrifying symbol of "the endless mad flux of things" (81) that threatens to overwhelm Faith with fast-moving, apparently unrelated experiences. Unlike the South, which threatens Faith with stasis, Chicago initially overwhelms her with accelerated, incoherent movement. Put another way, it resembles a classical underworld or a Christian hell, a "burial place" that "had invaded her, made her, shaped her wholly" (78).

Paradoxically, Faith's descent into this nether world plays a key role in her salvation. For the harsh realities of city life force her out of the extreme passivity that southern life necessitated and thus prod her into significant growth. Like Odysseus, Dante, and other epic heroes whose descents into underworlds enlarged their consciousness, Faith grows in self-knowledge as she moves through Chicago. And like Dante who is helped by Vergil to move through Hell toward Purgatory, Faith is assisted by mentors who keep her from being overwhelmed by the chaos she encounters. Curiously, one of her most valuable guides is Barrett, a man who had earlier victimized her when she first entered the city. Faith experiences a spiritual crisis that causes her to exclaim to him: "There isn't any good thing. There never was. It's all an evil lie to keep us happy! There's no thing . . . nothing" (89). Barrett saves her from a crippling nihilism centered in the conviction that "inner and outer worlds were . . . empty" (80) by reinstilling in her a belief in the "good thing" and her ability to pursue it. Outwardly "beaten" (85) and on the verge of death, Barrett becomes for Faith "not so much revolting but revelatory" (85). For it is he who reminds Faith that they are both "questers" (93) driven by a need to always search for the "tenuous belief" that "there had to be a greater good than any man could conceive" (90). He thus converts Faith from a disintegrating drifter into someone who can move with purpose, for it is he who commits her once again to "*the* human adventure, this quest for the Good Thing" (92).

It is Barrett who restores her faith in life as an open journey, for he convinces her that "The world was allegory . . . it always pointed beyond" (93). And it is he who gives her a powerful emblem of the plasticity and indeterminacy of human experience when he entrusts her with his Doomsday

Book, a book with blank pages inviting Faith to create her own self freely by writing the story of her life from scratch. Even though Barrett dies halfway through the novel, he continues to help Faith move meaningfully through life because his "philosopher's spirit" (98) continues to advise her whenever she is threatened with various kinds of traps. As she mechanically makes love to Maxwell in order to squeeze a proposal from him that will enslave them in a loveless marriage, she hears "Barrett's voice just above the wind telling her all this was horribly wrong" (109). At a later point when she fraudulently professes love to Maxwell, she envisions Barrett's face "frowning" (123) in disapproval. Whereas Maxwell is one of the "dead living" (125), Barrett is one of the "living dead" (125), a wise spirit who can caution Faith to resist such bondage. Like Dante's Vergil, he can return from the dead to provide a living voice which helps Faith in her journey. Indeed, he becomes a "wraith" or "conscience that would not let her rest" (96).

Barrett thus enables Faith to journey through Hell to Purgatory and, because of this, her experiences in Chicago do not damn her but purify her. Just as Dante is cleansed by the flames of Purgatory, which burn away the material drives that distract him from his spiritual quest, Faith undergoes a purification by fire when she is horribly disfigured by fire in Mrs. Beasely's hotel. The fire deprives her of the physical beauty that had earlier made it profitable for her to become a prostitute and had also drawn men like Tippis, Maxwell, and Holmes toward her. Deprived of her outward appearance, "her body seemed already gone, but her mind was clear" (183). And this mental clarity forces her to recognize the importance of burning away what is inessential in her life and committing herself once more to the "necessity" (183) for pursuing truth, the "Good Thing" (183).

It is precisely at this point that the Swamp Woman's white cat appears, inviting her to return "a long way home" (183) to Hatten County. There she will dedicate herself to the "Good Thing" by actually changing roles with the Swamp Woman. Her "odyssey" (184) therefore may be compared in some ways to the kind of journey that Joseph Campbell described in *The Hero with a Thousand Faces*. Like Campbell's archetypal hero, Faith begins her journey by responding to a "call to adventure"; she leaves the secure but stagnant world of Hatten County to pursue her quest for truth in Chicago. And Chicago is very much like the underworld into which Campbell's classical heroes descend to discover new powers that deepen their consciousness and enable them to experience a "life-enhancing return" home, resulting in "a vivid renewal of life."[2]

It would be misleading, however, to uncritically apply these parallels to Johnson's novel, seeing it as a neatly teleological narrative like Homer's *Odyssey*, Dante's *Commedia*, or Bunyan's *Pilgrim's Progress*. For Faith's journey does not end when she returns to the South; rather, it is just beginning. Indeed, the novel concludes with Faith equating placement with death and open movement with life. She rejects her father's invitation to join him in the world of the dead when he asks her if she wants to be completely immobilized by becoming a "maple tree" (178) like himself and her mother. Realizing that "she did not want to die" by becoming "sand, stone, perhaps a maple tree or an oak" (181), she strongly agrees with the Swamp Woman's conviction that all life is continuous motion. Even though she has elected to remain for a while *outwardly* stabilized in Hatten County, her inward life there is characterized by endless questing for truth, which she now realizes is always changing, never resting. Her life therefore is an open journey that requires her to "take every path" and "keep right on steppin'" (187). Realizing the wisdom of the Swamp Woman's statement that "on every path you'll find a li'l bit of the Good Thing" (194), Faith now sees her life as an endless series of paths leading her to an indefinite number of truths. Realizing this, she undergoes a powerful conversion experience that enables her to see all reality in Emersonian terms as an endless process of becoming:

> Confused, Faith pulled back the thin curtain of the window (it *was*, she realized, made of skin—great strips sewn together with human hair). Light burst in thin blue beams that caused her to blink, opening and closing her eyes until she could see. It was dawn, a time that had always taken hold of something in her blood; dawn, a new beginning; dawn, a moment both still and serene, suggesting that her long night of questioning had been quite unreal. Around the shanty, coming in waves from the swamp, was the sustained orchestration of songbirds: hooting, cooing, chirping, squawking, and crying on the unseen undercurrent of the wind. . . . She saw an elm tree towering over the other trees in the distance, waving its highest branches in the breeze. Todd Cross. She was certain. Certain of everything. Certain the air was cool and scented with the clean smell of dew. Certain the wind pushed on, and the birds swung into the empty sky like sleek arrows, no destination, no duty, no destiny in mind. (193–94)

By the end of the novel, therefore, Faith thinks of her life as having the free and indeterminate rhythms of nature. Just as the sun rises every day to produce a new dawn, her protean self will always have a "new beginning," new possibilities for limitless growth. The "waves" of song from the birds and the "undercurrent of the wind" provide her with compelling evidence that nothing in nature is static and that her life ought to be as free as the birds who fly with no "destination . . . no destiny in mind." Like the wind, her life "pushed on."

Thus envisioning her life as an open journey, she also imagines the self in protean terms as continuous development, ongoing metamorphoses:

> She'd suffered several roles: the innocent, the whore, the housewife. And now, the werewitch herself. There would be others. There had to be. She was more than any one path, or the total of them all. She would glean from each its store of the Good Thing, would conjure it up: the enthusiasm and naivete of youth, the self-sacrifice of the streetwalker, and the love that even the most miserable housewife received—exhausting them, moving on to another path, and another. . . . And when she traveled the existing paths, she would create a new untrodden one. That was progress. If she discovered X number of paths and traveled them all, then she, before she died, would leave X-plus-1. That was responsibility: factoring the possible number of paths to the Good Thing, but not becoming fixed, or held to those paths in her history, or the history of the race. Moving always on. . . . (195)

Realizing that her life will be "Moving always on" because she will never become restricted, as was her mother, to "one path" in life, she knows that the self is fluid and multiple, containing an indefinite number of possibilities. Hence her return to the South is quite different from Celie's return to Georgia at the end of *The Color Purple*. Whereas Celie completes her identity by rooting herself in a definite place that connects her to a specific culture with definite values, Faith returns home "on a temporary visa" (185) and, like the Swamp Woman, reserves the right to leave the South at any time. As she has discovered earlier, Hatten County no longer exists for her as an actual place that can define her present life, since her parents are dead, her homestead burned down, and "There was nothing left of her old life" (133). What she does return to temporarily is a liminal space by a swamp on the outskirts of southern society where she can freely conjure without fear of being bothered by southern whites, who lynched her father when he rejected his assigned place in a racist society. By the end of the novel Faith has rejected altogether the idea of place, instead inhabiting an imaginative space that empowers her with the Swamp Woman's magical ability to "change herself into anything she damn well pleased" (159). The swamp therefore is similar to the invisible man's underground room, a confining place transformed by the power of imagination and will into a liberating space large enough to accommodate the hero's need for constant growth.

Faith's open journey resembles the free outward and inward movements of the Swamp Woman but is sharply contrasted with the journeys undertaken by every other character in the novel. Her free but purposeful motion, for example, should not be equated with the random movements that characterize Tippis, Lynch, and Holmes. Dr. Lynch, for example, experiences his life as he sees the universe, as a series of accidental movements. Just as he sees the world in grimly entropic terms as Brownian movement ending merely in death ("Life brings death" [37]), he imagines his own experiences as having neither purpose nor direction and eventually commits suicide. Tippis's early life may be seen in a comparable way. His "plastic personality" (83) is the product of other people imposing a random series of identities upon him that are essentially meaningless. Although he wanted as a boy to become a "travelling musician" (60), the aunt who raised him destroyed this ambition by breaking his hands with a poker, forcing him to plan a more "respectable" life for himself. The remainder of his life has consisted of his bouncing back and forth between a number of roles that others choose for him: dentist, porter, salesman, and male nurse. Because "Tippis's changes were never from within, only catalyzed from without" (83), his life is meaningless movement resulting in despair. Holmes, although more independent than Tippis and not given to despair like Lynch, nevertheless leads an unfulfilling life as a drifter. Even though his free movements stimulate him as an artist, his extreme "restlessness" is finally seen as a "disease" (167) when he refuses to acknowledge himself as the father of Faith's child and abandons her by taking off for New York. Because he absolutely refuses to "let this thing tie me down" (166) and is unable to enter a "new path" in life by becoming a father, he too is finally seen as one of the "dead living" (167) who urges Faith to have an abortion.

Faith's movements are radically free and open, but they are not random like the movements that characterize the lives of Lynch, Tippis, and Holmes; they are purposely driven by her search for truth. To emphasize this, Johnson repeatedly describes her life as having "rhythm," a free and natural pattern that endows her experiences with coherence and direction. As a girl she moves toward a "vision of complete freedom" (12) that is as natural to her as her "own heartbeat" (12). Making love to Holmes, she feels in unison with the grass and trees, thinking that their "pulsations" bring the two of them in line with the "single heartbeat of the universe" (13). (Later she regards his abandonment of her as "suffocating" them before the "rhythm of the world" [167].) Even at the traumatic moment when she is raped by Tippis, she is revived by the feel of her "rhythmic" (63) breathing, which corresponds to the music being played next door. Likewise, when she passes out after an argument with Maxwell, she is refreshed by dreaming of "a green meadow ringing with earth rhythms" (127). Because Faith instinctively believes "reality is simply a rhythm" (139–40), the motions of her life have a loose, natural design that infuses these movements with purpose and direction. She thus is sharply contrasted with characters like Lynch, Tippis, and Holmes, who, to various degrees, are condemned to lives of empty drifting.

Furthermore, she is contrasted with people who conceive of life in terms of rigidly mechanical movements. Maxwell, for example, trivializes human experience by envisioning it as an immense football game whose movements are controlled by sharply defined markers and whose purpose is to move to a definite place called the "end zone" where "points" can be scored that enable one to "win." He thus regards the great moment of "revelation" (116) in his life as watching the Rose Bowl and then imagining his life as a triumphant football game in which he repeatedly crosses the goal line to score points. This crude metaphor reduces everything to a neat but empty routine that he rigidly controls. Given such a simplistic and amoral worldview, he can easily justify forcing his wife to going to bed with one of his bosses, viewing such an act as "carrying the ball" (136) for him on his football field of success. Although Faith's performance helps to win a promotion for Maxwell, it reduces her once again to the condition of a slave in "bondage" (112).

She likewise feels enslaved by conventional religions that portray the human journey in mechanistic terms. Reverend Magnus tells her that she must move step by step toward a clearly defined heaven or sink to the pit of an equally well defined hell. Such a vision "froze" (11) Faith and makes her feel "trapped in a room full of mirrors" (12). Faith also feels confined by the religious vision she receives when attending a service at the Church of the Continual Light. Although this religious belief offers her "a security she longed to have" (73), she rejects it because she feels that its rigorously teleological outlook is "a one-way street" (78); its members can only move in one preconceived direction. For the minister perceives religious truth as something that must be accepted by a changeless authority rather than something which must be personally struggled for in a world of flux:

> Can't you see how *horrible* it is to be separated by all the universe from the thing we need most? Only one step remained: to look inside ourselves—to put it so close we don't have to search all over the world no more! The minister tapped his chest, then smacked it hard. "It's in here! That's the only place it is, or could ever be—in your hearts!" (74)

Faith rejects this sort of fundamentalist religion because it absolutizes truth by embedding it in a "place" that can be reached after a "final step" is made. She instinctively pulls back from such a simplistic and static view of truth, assigning it to the realm of "memory" (75) to which she can no longer relate. She instead commits herself to the sometimes confusing but always challenging flux of the present, seeing truth as forever changing, always acquiring new shapes.

Because of this nearly instinctive drive for open motion, Faith keeps alive the most deeply human part of her, the inward self that transcends both time and place. Throughout the novel she is described as having two selves, a rigid outer part that is trapped by the accidents of history and society and a fluid inner part that has the potential for indefinite growth. As she is being raped by Tippis, she becomes acutely aware of this duality:

> She lay perfectly rigid, tight-lipped like a corpse with rusty pennies on its eyes—praying. No one, apparently, had heard. For Tippis continued, his lips humming, and in his mouth was a gurgling sound. Faith twisted her head and vomited over the side of the bed, no longer praying now, but thinking, "To me . . . not to *me* is this happening." Not to that well-protected portion of herself that came spinning forth whenever she said, "I . . . me . . . myself," not to her, but to some part other than herself, some weak and vulnerable part that so easily could be made an object, that was incapable of escaping circumstance and chance. To herself she whispered, "This is *bad*, Faith. Bad . . . Faith." The darkness helped. She couldn't see him, or what he was doing, and it was easy to dam her ears to his breathing by shouting deep within her mind again and again:
> "I am Faith Cross . . .
> "I am Faith . . .
> "I *am* . . .
> "I . . . ?" (61–62)

Whereas her outer self is described here in terms of stasis—it "lay perfectly rigid" on the bed and is reduced to the status of an acted-upon "object," her inward self is described in terms of free movement, for it is capable of "escaping circumstance and chance" whenever it comes "spinning forth." Faith's external self, which is described here as a corpse with pennies on its eyes, is trapped throughout the novel when she becomes an "object" that people like Tippis exploit. But her inner self—presented here as an "I" that she literally distills from her innermost feelings and thoughts—moves forward in life, preserving her integrity and making possible her growth. Even when she is outwardly degraded by her condition as a whore, her inward self reminds her that "She was Faith Cross with such and such possibilities" (69). While her customers treat her like a passive object, she knows deeply within herself that she is a self-propelling subject who can pursue important "possibilities."

Her relationships with Barrett and Maxwell also vividly illustrate her duality. Even though her material self almost perversely seeks the trap that Maxwell sets for her, the spiritual self at the core of her being is strongly attracted to Barrett, a vagrant whose physical life is little more than "wreckage" (93) but whose interior life keeps him questing for the "elusive Good Thing" (95) that humanizes him. Drawn between these two poles, she leads "a deceitful double life" (164), poised between Maxwell, whose soul is "still as a stone" (125), and Barrett, who even in death continues to grow in Faith's consciousness. Appropriately, his grave is described as a spot where "flowers might yet bloom" (95).

By the end of the novel Faith consciously rejects that part of her which links her to the "dead living" and endorses that part of her which naturally gravitates toward motion and life. The fire in the Hotel Sinclair that horribly disfigures her body destroys her faith in the outer self but it purifies her inner being, so that she can finally tell Maxwell to "*Go* away!" (182). She then puts herself in motion, leaving the dark underworld of Chicago and moving to the magical universe of the Swamp Woman, where she undergoes a metamorphosis that moves her closer to the Good Thing.

Like many American and African American picaresque heroes, Faith is saved by an open journey that allows her to transcend both time and place. She finally tramps Whitman's "perpetual journey"[3] toward the "infinite possibilities"[4] that Ellison speaks of in *Invisible Man*. Even in her worst moments when she feels "placed" with the "label" of a whore" (65), she still has recourse to an existential self that is not a changeless "essence" (65) but an open process shaped by acts of free will and imagination, what Johnson calls "freedom and . . . magical thinking" (65). It is this protean self that enables her to push forward, "moving always on" (195) to new spaces that liberate her. Like Huck Finn, she is rejuvenated by the "territory ahead,"[5] and like Frederick Douglass she is able to propel herself away from a condition of slavery. Although early in the novel she imagines herself as trapped by a slave past that is "final, irreversible" (65), and actually summarizes her entire life with a terrifying image of her being picked up by the slave ship *The Trinity*, she finally uses consciousness and will heroically to transform her life, liberating herself from bondage of any kind.

All of Johnson's work since the publication of *Faith and the Good Thing* in 1974 has flowed from this belief in life as an open journey and the self as a protean matrix of limitless possibilities. In *Being and Race* (1988) he insists that

> We find meaning in flux, on the side of Heraclitus (change) and not Parmenides (stasis); we find, I am saying, the black world *overflowing* with meaning, so rich and multisided that literally anything—and everything—can be found there, good and bad, and one of the first chores of the writer is to be immersed in this embarrassment of rich, contradictory material.

Because of this, he is opposed to any "calcified ways of seeing" that would reduce the fertile, always growing matrix of black experience to rigid systems or categories that do violence to the dynamic complexity of black life by oversimplifying it and arresting its growth. He therefore sees himself as a "protean writer" who is receptive to the fluid, indeterminate nature of reality and can express this vision in a variety of flexible forms. Deeply committed to the idea that "the language is not fixed but evolving" and "all literary forms are evolving," he sees himself as a fabulist who transforms experience rather than as a realist or naturalist who statically "records" life and thus freezes experience.[6]

The main task of Johnson's central characters therefore is to overcome the "slavery" brought on by rigid modes of perception and to free themselves with inward and outward journeys to open spaces inviting self-creation. The hero of *Oxherding Tales*, for example, disdains the crippling fictions that others have invented to blunt his mind and blur his vision. He then sets about the crucial task of "reinventing [his] biography" from his own angle of vision so that he may destroy his old life as the slave Andrew Hawkins and create a new life as the freed man William Harris. Such a process of self-creation sets him upon a journey that is liberatingly open, driven by possibilities in the future rather than a given identity from the past:

> Whatever my origin, I would be wholly responsible for the shape I gave
> myself in the future, shirting myself with a new life that called me like a
> siren to possibilities that were real but forever out of reach.

Allured by such possibilities, which are "real" but "forever out of reach,"
he embraces his life as an open journey—endless movement through "new
territory" that is "without a map."[7]

In the same way, Rutherford Calhoun, the hero of *Middle Passage*
(1990) freely creates a protean identity in a slave society that tries to fix
him in a "place" denying him human growth. Like Melville's Ishmael, he
leaves the world of "land" that threatens to enslave him and sets out on
"the open, endless sea" in a metaphysical journey that transforms his consciousness and gives him a new identity. Claiming that "The voyage had
irreversibly changed my seeing," he comes to understand that the human
self is not a "Parmenidean meaning" but "Heraclitan change." Armed with
this knowledge, he agrees with Captain Falcon that slavery is "the social
correlate of a deeper ontic wound . . . a transcendental fault, a deep crack in
consciousness itself." His open journey heals him of this wound, allowing
him to develop the sort of dynamic consciousness he needs to emancipate
himself from slavery in all of its forms. Like Ellison's invisible man, from
whom he clearly descends, he compares himself to "Odysseus" (207), the
protean hero who can master ever-changing reality with a supple consciousness that is as creative as life itself.[8]

6

Ishmael Reed's *Flight to Canada:* Artistic Process as Endless Voyage

> Jes Grew has no end and no beginning . . . Jes Grew is life.
> —*Mumbo Jumbo*

Whereas *Faith and the Good Thing* defines the African American open journey in metaphysical terms as an endless dialectic providing a multiplicity of ever-evolving truths that can be the basis for a protean identity, Ishmael Reed's *Flight to Canada* defines this quest in metafictional terms as the artistic process itself. Reed's novel, like all metafictions, is artfully self-reflexive; that is, it examines the story-making process in an intricately self-conscious way as its central subject. Like Beckett's *The Unnamable*, Barth's *Lost in the Funhouse*, and Coover's *Pricksongs and Descants*, *Flight to Canada* is "writing about writing," discussing how it is being formed as a story and using the fiction-making process as a basic metaphor of how people perceive the world and shape their identities. Self-creation, then, is a process of discovering and then telling one's own "stories," all the while revising or rejecting the fictions that others have invented for their own needs. In this sense, the narrator of James Alan McPherson's *Elbow Room* envisions himself as "a work of art"[1] because he has fashioned his own identity; he imagines himself in positive terms rather than according to the debilitating fictions imposed upon him by white people who attempt to fix him within the stereotype of "nigger." The hero of Johnson's *Oxherding Tales*, likewise, considers his essential task as "reinventing [his] biography,"[2] that is, saying no to the stories others have constructed to enslave him and then fashioning a richly protean identity for himself as he envisions his life as a series of stories that he is free to create.

For Reed, the artistic process resulting in such self-creation is a radically open journey. In *Mumbo Jumbo* (1972) he uses the term "Jes Grew" as a trope for artistic process, stressing its indeterminate, protean qualities, what he describes as its "liquidity." It moves with "no definite route" and, indeed, "has no end and no beginning." "Wiggling wobbling rambling and shambling," it goes "Any which way" as it is "seeking its words, its text." Reed therefore imagines artistic creation as a dynamic process that is always moving in unpredictable ways, dissolving fixed modes of perceiving reality and empowering people to perceive themselves and their world in fresh new ways. As such, it resists categorization of any kind: "It is nothing we can bring into focus or categorize; once we call it 1 thing it forms into something else." In its most general terms, "Jes Grew is life," a protean force whose energies are always assuming new forms, transforming fixed reality into fluid possibility.[3]

As such, the artistic process is the enemy of slavery in all of its forms, especially as they persist for blacks in contemporary American life. Novels such as *Oxherding Tales*, *Faith and the Good Thing,* and *Flight to Canada* envision slavery as continuing to threaten blacks long after it has ceased to exist as an actual social institution, because the "stories" that whites have told about blacks to justify slavery persist and continue to affect economic, political, and social reality in America. As Hazel Carby has observed,

> [S]lavery haunts the literary imagination because its material conditions and social relations are frequently reproduced in fiction as historically dynamic; they continue to influence society long after emancipation. The economic and social system of slavery is thus a pre-history (as well as a pre-text to all Afro-American texts), a past social condition that can explain contemporary phenomena.[4]

Just as Johnson's Faith Cross is threatened by various forms of "bondage" in the twentieth century, Reed asks the question in *Flight to Canada* "Was there no end to slavery?"[5] To give a vivid sense of how certain aspects of nineteenth-century slavery survive in contemporary American life, Reed anachronistically mixes modern reality with what seems to be a pre–Civil War setting. Hence Quickskill can use a Texas Instruments calculator in his job as bookkeeper on Swille's plantation. Likewise, Uncle Robin can watch television while lying on a water bed in the slave quarters and Mrs. Swille, the mistress of the plantation, can enjoy *The Beecher Hour* on her color television.

For Reed, modern American slavery has its deepest roots in the linguistic disempowerment of blacks, something that dates back to their earliest days on the American continent when they were cut off from their native languages and separated from their oral literature, which provided them with stories that defined their values as black people. Hence they were put at the mercy of a new language that whites controlled and narratives that expressed the values of the dominant culture. This linguistic disempowerment not only forced blacks into demeaning social roles created by whites but also psychologically limited black thought and development through what Kimberly Benston has called "enslaving fictions."[6] For example, the Bible gave whites enormous social and psychological leverage over blacks, since it was filled with narratives like the story of Ham that whites could use to justify their harsh treatment of slaves. Because blacks were separated from traditional African narratives that could provide them with affirmative, even heroic, images of themselves that countered the degrading stereotypes generated by white culture, they were victimized by the "stories" whites told about them in order to immobilize them as slaves.

Even a writer like Harriet Beecher Stowe, whose *Uncle Tom's Cabin* was a well-intentioned attempt to end slavery by telling the story of its injustices and brutality, is seen by Reed as part of the problem, not part of the solution. For in writing her novel Stowe performed a literary act of enslavement, stealing the story of a black man named Josiah Henson just as slave traders had literally stolen slaves from their native land. The net result was to create a master text filled with stereotypical images of black people that persist in the popular imagination to the present day. As Reed sees it, Stowe's expropriation of a black text ironically helped to prolong slavery rather than end it, for it substituted an enslaving white text for a liberating black text:

> She'd read Josiah Henson's book. That Harriet was alert. The Life of Josiah Henson. *Seventy pages long. It was short but it was his. It was all he had. His story. A man's story is his gris-gris, you know. Taking his story is like taking his gris-gris. The thing that is himself.* (8)

The writing of Henson's story made Stowe a world-famous writer and also a wealthy woman who used her money to build what Reed calls "a Virginia plantation in New England" (9), but it did little to help Henson, who died "hopeless and frustrated" (8) in economic slavery, ironically after escaping to Canada in search of his freedom.

Describing modern American slavery as blacks being imprisoned by the "stories" that whites have constructed about them, Reed writes his own literary Emancipation Proclamation in *Flight to Canada*. His novel is an attempt to tell the story of blacks in America from the time of slavery to the present, but to tell it from a distinctively black perspective. In order to do this, he employs a traditional form of African American journey literature, the slave narrative, but frees it from white control. Whereas most of the nineteenth-century slave narratives were directed at a white audience, edited by a white editor, and introduced by a white abolitionist who would verify the "authenticity" of the text, Reed consciously purges these conventions from a black text by ironically inverting some of the conventions of traditional slave narratives.

Flight to Canada thus opens up with a black poem that completely subverts the standard expectations of the introduction usually found in nineteenth-century slave narratives. While the white abolitionist writing an introduction usually took pains to reassure a white audience that the slave who wrote the narrative was a devout Christian who could responsibly rebel against a condition of slavery within a "Christian" framework acceptable to whites, Reed's novel opens with a poem written by a much less manageable black rebel who wants to poison his master after drinking his best liquor, stealing his money, and sleeping with his "prime Quadroon" (9). Far from the penniless slave eagerly seeking white support usually depicted in the introductions to slave narratives, Reed's runaway slave roars into Canada on a jumbo jet, "Travelling in style" (3). Using money he has made from his *own* writing, he drinks champagne as he arranges a series of profitable antislavery lectures.

The actual journeys envisioned by Reed's novel and traditional slave narratives are also ironically contrasted with each other in certain ways. Although both take the form of flight from a condition of servitude in the South to a kind of liberation in the North, Reed's novel expresses a radical disillusionment with any actual places outside the South. Whereas, for example, a fugitive slave such as Frederick Douglass had enough faith in America to believe that there was some real place such as Rochester, New York, or New Bedford, Massachusetts, that could provide him with a "home," Reed depicts all *places* as various kinds of betrayals. The journey in Reed's novel, therefore, is completely nonteleological, a search for open space rather than movement directed toward a particular place. The "Canada" to which the hero moves, therefore, is a psychological condition rather than a precise location in external reality. As Robin declares at the end of the novel, "Well I guess Canada, like freedom, is a state of mind" (178).

All actual places in *Flight to Canada* disappoint Quickskill and his friends. When he goes to Buffalo he is beaten up by racists who object to his antislavery speeches. Taking up residence later in a place called Emancipation City, which is somewhere near the Great Lakes, he is nearly "repossessed" (62) by bounty hunters called Nebraska Tracers who are paid to return him to Swille's plantation. Emancipation City, created by a pirate named Yankee Jack to make huge profits for himself, is no model of American freedom but is instead another version of the slave society that Quickskill thinks he has escaped. Jack's sumptuous "castle" (94) calls to mind the "castle" that Quickskill's owner built in Virginia, and the main shopping mall in Emancipation City, called Pirates Plaza, is modeled after "the slave fort built by Europeans on the coast of New Guinea" (94). Furthermore, the most prominent gathering place for ex-slaves is called the "Slave Hole Cafe" (67), yet another version of the conditions endured by slaves during the Middle Passage. Leechfield escapes one form of slavery in Virginia only to be reenslaved in Emancipation City, where he performs in Leer's pornographic films and advertises himself in local newspapers as "Your Slave for One Day" (80). Quickskill endures a milder but still humiliating form of slavery in Emancipation City when he becomes a kind of "house nigger" while watching the house of vacationing abolitionists.

Quickskill's dreams of freedom are sustained by his reading books about Canada, a country he romanticizes as being run by a liberal House of Commons and presided over by a prime minister whom he sees as "the most enlightened man in the Western world" (69). But after crossing the Niagara River into Canada, he finds the same forms of slavery from which he is trying to escape. Ironically, he goes to Niagara Falls, Ontario, where the falls themselves become an obvious metaphor of disaster, a "downfall" he will almost certainly experience if he stays in such a place. Niagara Falls, Ontario turns out to be a cheap carbon copy of Niagara Falls, New York, a grossly commercialized world where everything is reduced to its dollar value. Even though Quickskill at first perceives the Canadian Falls as "the closest spot to heaven on earth" because "People of all races, classes, and descriptions seemed to be there," beholding the falls in "wonder" (157), he is soon disillusioned by what he observes. His friend Carpenter, a free Negro, is denied a room in a hotel because he is black and is then beaten up by "mobocrats" (159) when he complains about such treatment. A Klan-like group called "The Western Guard" (160) is based in nearby St. Catherines, Ontario, and is fanatically committed to preserving white domination of Canada. When Quickskill tries to reassure Carpenter that Canada is, despite these flaws, a better place for blacks than the United States, his friend tells him, "Man, as soon as you reach the metropolitan areas you run into Ford, Sears, Holiday Inns, and the rest" (160). Carpenter then equates the United States and Canada when he declares in exasperation, "Americans own Canada" (161). Just as Johnson's Faith Cross leaves the South only to be reenslaved by northern forms of commercial exploitation, Quickskill finds himself in a Canadian society that not only threatens blacks physically with violence but, more importantly, endangers them spiritually with a commercialism that once more reduces them to the level of things. It is no surprise, therefore, that Quickskill soon becomes "depressed" (161) about Canada and eventually leaves.

But even though Canada as a physical place at the end of a teleological journey proves to be a bitter disappointment, Quickskill's "flight to Canada" is reaffirmed on another level as the sort of open journey celebrated in African American novels such as Ellison's *Invisible Man* and Walker's *The Third Life of Grange Copeland*. As a "state of mind" taking the form of symbolic open space, Canada offers Quickskill the psychological room he needs to achieve a life of freedom and independence. Quickskill ultimately realizes that he can make a "way out of no way" by moving in the liberating spaces of his creative imagination rather than the restrictive places he has known:

> He preferred Canada to slavery whether Canada was exile, death, art, liberation or a woman. Each man to his own Canada. There was much avian imagery in the poetry of slaves. Poetry about dreams and flight. They wanted to cross that Black Rock Ferry to freedom even though they had different notions as to what freedom was. (88)

"Exile" and "a woman" fail him when his lover Quaw Quaw deserts him so that she can be freer to pursue what she hopes is a lucrative career as a tightrope walker. But this does not leave him with the bleak alternative of "death," since "liberation" in the form of "art" is still available to him. He finally envisions Canada in literary terms as a space in the imagination, promising the radical freedom necessary for selfhood, and he knows that he can "move" to such a world through the process of artistic creation: "[I]t was his writing that got him to Canada . . . his typewriter was the drum he danced to" (89). Just as Thoreau's Walden is not merely a place in the woods but a symbol of the vast, uncharted spaces of his mind, and just as Ellison's hole beneath the streets of Harlem is not a confining place but instead an objective correlative to the limitless spaces of his imagination, Reed's "Canada" is not a place on a map but a metaphor of the indeterminate possibilities of artistic creation. In this sense Swille is clearly wrong when he cynically claims, "That nigger ain't in no Canada. There ain't no such place. That's reactionary mysticism" (52). By rejecting Swille's literal language and transforming Canada into a symbol, Quickskill emancipates language from white domination, converting a term of betrayal and enslavement into a term of black liberation.

The artistic process, therefore, is for Reed the real journey from slavery to freedom. It is in art that blacks can reclaim the "story" expropriated by well-meaning whites such as Harriet Beecher Stowe who helped to enslave them with the clichés of the sentimental novel and not-so-well-intended whites who helped to enslave blacks with the stereotypical fictions of the Plantation School. In writing their own stories independent of the racist conceptions of white writers and their audiences, black writers like Quickskill can reenvision history and thus create imaginative space in which blacks can transcend their "places" and create their own identities. Quickskill believes that a "thing" may be turned into an "I am" by "Tons of paper" (82), for writing produces consciousness, which dissolves the stereotypes that freeze blacks into dehumanizing roles and empowers them to fashion their own selves in a free, open way. Throughout the novel, therefore, words are given the magical quality of putting the self in motion after it has been paralyzed by a condition of slavery. Just as traditional slave narratives regarded the achievement of literacy as a crucial act because it opened the mind to the evils of slavery and enabled the slave to imagine alternatives to slavery and thus take the first steps on the road to freedom, reading and writing for Quickskill allow him to break out of the prison of slavery and undertake an open journey to freedom and selfhood. As the narrator tells us, "Raven was the first one of Swille's slaves to read, the first one to write and the first to run away" (14). Although Swille allows Quickskill to achieve literacy in order to become his "trusted bookkeeper" (35) who will write and manage the documents used to enslave people, Quickskill uses his literacy to do his *own* writing, subversively destroying contracts, forging passes, and writing freedom papers. Swille discovers the connection between literacy and mobility too late, complaining that Raven's skill as a reader and writer of documents has seriously undermined his slave society. Worse, many other slaves on his plantation have also "taken to writing" (34) and are now "pass[ing] codes to one another" (34).

Quickskill writes two poems, and each one puts him more firmly on the road to freedom. For in creatively using his own words, he can emancipate himself from the language of white society which fixes him in restrictive roles. In "The Saga of the Third World Belle" he imagines himself thusly:

> . . . I am a native mind riding
> Bareback, backwards through
> a wood of words and when I stumble
> I get my Ibo up and hobble
> like a bloody-footed slave
> Traveling from Virginia to

> Ohio and if I stumble again
> I get my Cherokee up and smell
> My way to the clearing.
>
>   (123–24)

His writing here puts him in free motion, riding "bareback" on a horse galloping through a "wood of words." Riding backwards enables him to sharply reverse the direction whites have given him. He can thus clearly see the past he is leaving but has some difficulty envisioning the future toward which he aspires. Nevertheless, he stumbles through such a verbal "wood" and eventually finds a free space or "clearing." Such free movement likens him to a fugitive slave finally reaching the free state of Ohio or Ibo warriors, fiercely proud African natives who refused to be enslaved by whites.

"Flight to Canada," the poem that prefaces the novel, also depicts Quickskill as moving toward freedom and selfhood. Written initially to taunt his master, it describes Quickskill dramatically entering the free space of Canada on a jumbo jet after performing a "Liza Leap" (3) out of slave territory. Like Stowe's Liza who jumps from ice floe to ice floe to finally cross the Ohio River into free territory, he has magically avoided his tormentors and is at last free. Although the poem is an imaginative act and was written several years prior to his actually entering Canada, the act of writing the poem has put him in motion in two important ways: it has given him the power to confront and torment his master and the slave world he represents; and it has provided him royalties, which eventually pay for his boat ride across the Niagara River into Canada. For these reasons, Quickskill savors the thought that "'Flight to Canada' had gotten him to Canada" (88–89). Writing has both mentally liberated him and given him the financial independence he needs to translate into action his dreams of moving into free space. It is in this sense that "Freedom was his writing" (89).

Words therefore have enormous power for Quickskill. When his friend 40's asks him, "What good is words?," he answers, "Words built the world and words can destroy the world" (81). Reed's novel provides several examples of how words have been used to build up restrictive worlds that destroy human beings by fixing them in crudely stereotypical roles. The Swilles base their slave society in part on their perverse reading of the Arthurian legends, building what they think is a new version of Camelot but which in fact is a "Wasp's Jerusalem" (15), a society that Calvinistically enslaves thousands of the "damned" in order to privilege a few of the "elect." And Stowe's Uncle Tom's Cabin promises to destroy the old world of slavery but in fact further enslaves blacks by locking them into rigid stereotypes that persist in the popular imagination to current times. (Significantly, both of these works from white tradition envision closed journeys; the Arthurian quest ends in a place called Camelot, a hierarchical world that places all people in social classes, and Stowe's journey ends in a neatly defined domestic "home" that also assigns a fixed social role to each individual.)

But *Flight to Canada* is premised upon an open journey that frees its characters from the restrictive roles imagined in books like *Morte D'Arthur* and *Uncle Tom's Cabin*. It therefore celebrates the salvific function of words, supplying many examples of how people can imaginatively dismantle the fictions that help to enslave them and can then use words creatively to liberate themselves. Quickskill can use his writing in a number of liberating ways, first of all by forging freedom papers for himself and others and then writing a novel that will not only counter the myth of Camelot and Uncle Tom but will construct a potently mythic image of "Canada" as a free space. In a similar way, Robin will secure freedom from slavery when he shrewdly rewrites Swille's will, thus acquiring ownership over a world that has previously owned him.

Because they have finally assumed power over the words that have previously dominated them and because they have emphatically rejected the fictions that have previously been used to enslave them, the novel's major black characters finally transcend the "place" that American society has assigned them and achieve the open space that they need in order to move freely toward identities that they create for themselves. At the end of the novel Judy asks Robin, who has inherited Swille's plantation, "What are you going to do with all this space?" (179), and he answers, "I am going to take this fifty rooms of junk and turn it into something useful" (179). We know from the beginning of the novel, which is set in a time postdating the ending of the novel, that Robin has converted the plantation into a school, which is dedicated to helping people to grow by more fully realizing their human potential. The "blacksmiths, teachers, sculptors, writers" (10) who have replaced masters, slaves, and overseers will indeed enable Robin to create something useful out of his inheritance, for each is a kind of artist helping to transform people's lives from a condition of slavery to the creation of new possibilities. Now that the plantation is no longer a slave society but a school devoted to liberating people, Quickskill can return there to play a number of important roles. He is given the entire first floor of the castle and enjoys its ample space ("It was airy and had big spacious rooms" [11]) as a setting for artistic creation. He starts his new life by writing a book that tells Robin's story but he is careful not to use Stowe's methods:

> Quickskill would write Uncle Robin's story in such a way that, using a
> process the old curers used, to lay hands on the story would be lethal to
> the thief. That way his Uncle Robin would have the protection that Uncle
> Tom (Josiah Henson) didn't. (11)

Such writing effects "curing" in two ways. First of all, it preserves Robin's
actual history without misunderstanding it, falsifying it, or using it for
another's advantage, as did Stowe's pilfering of Henson's story. Secondly,
Quickskill's storytelling "cures" Robin in the sense that it helps to heal the
damage done to him by slavery, a social system based in pathological
fictions. Before Quickskill returns to the castle, Robin feels that he is too
old to escape the "prison" (178) of his life and thinks that his dream of
"Canada" is no longer possible for him. As he tells his wife Judy, "I couldn't
go for no Canada . . . I done had my Canadas" (178). But Raven Quickskill
as an artist can help Robin to overcome this static vision of his life by
telling Robin's story truly and helping him to convert a plantation (a static
place that fixes people in roles) into a school (a dynamic space that helps
people to grow). As a result, Robin has stopped his stereotypical shuffling
and put himself into motion: "He and Judy travelled a lot. Now they were
in the Ashanti Holy Land" (11). Refusing to let whites write a "book" (174)
about him, he has returned to Africa to understand the sacred stories that
blacks have fashioned for themselves. As his name suggests, Robin is a
spring bird who, despite his years, is still capable of "flying."

Raven Quickskill's name is also a key to his protean identity. Because
of his quickness and skill as an artist, he can free himself of the verbal
constructs and inhibiting roles imposed upon him by white society. And
because "A raven is always on the move" (144), he will not become trapped
by the fictions that have immobilized others, whether these fictions take
the form of Swille's grandiose dreams of being a new King Arthur presid-
ing over Camelot or Quaw Quaw's lesser dream of becoming a new Blondin,
the first woman to walk a tightrope successfully over the Niagara Gorge.
Even though Quickskill's journey literally results in his migrating back to
Virginia, this is no longer the static place that had earlier enslaved him. Just
as Ellison's hero can turn an underground room into a womb and Johnson's
Faith Cross can transform a southern swamp into a magical locus for self-
creation, Quickskill finally transfigures a restrictive place into a liberating
space, his Canada of the mind.

While metafictionists such as Samuel Beckett, John Barth, and Robert Coover often use self-reflexive fiction nihilistically to suggest that the self has no meaning apart from the arbitrary and solipsistic creations of depleted imaginations on the verge of collapse, black metafictionists such as Clarence Major, Charles Johnson, and Ishmael Reed use postmodern fictional experiments affirmatively, often seeing the creative process as an open journey with limitless possibilities. The reason for this is that white and black metafictionists regard the literary traditions from which they spring in strikingly opposite ways. Novelists like Beckett and Barth often complain that they feel enervated by being part of a literary tradition that has become overly formalized and lacks fresh stories to tell. But African American metafictionists regard their own literary tradition as a potent source of literary creation, since it is bursting with old stories to untell and new stories to tell, stories that until recently were stifled by a white-dominated reading public and neglected by black writers, who were taught to undervalue their own folk and literary traditions.

In a way that has come to typify the enervated voice of much white experimental fiction, for example, the narrator of Beckett's *The Unnamable* complains that the story of his life has been meaningless, since it is based on trivialized "lies" and takes the form of a journey that dissolves into nothingness:

> I invented it all in the hope it would console me, help me to go on, allow me to think of myself as somewhere on a road, moving, between a beginning and an end, gaining ground, losing ground, but somehow in the long run making headway. All lies. I have nothing to do. I have to speak, whatever that means. Having nothing to say, no words but the words of others . . . there is nothing, nothing to discover, nothing to recover. . . .

Sensing that his language is not his own but the "words of others," Beckett can find no meanings in his life either to "discover" or "recover." His life therefore takes the form of a journey disintegrating into oblivion, having no direction or coherence and making no "headway." Envisioning his life as meaningless movement, what he calls "labyrinthine torment" (314), he longs for stasis, a mind-numbing paralysis.[7]

In sharp contrast, a black metafictionist such as James Alan McPherson sees the creative process in very affirmative terms as a postmodern equivalent to traditional American westering, since it supplies him with the psychological and imaginative "elbow room" that gives his characters the free space they need for self-creation rather than giving them "lies." As he says

of one of his major characters, "She had inside her an epic adventure, inter-
national in scope."[8] The resources within her fertile imagination create limitless possibilities just as the epic West had given classic American heroes
indefinite possibilities for new lives. In a similar way, the story-making
process offers the hero of *Oxherding Tales* ways of breaking free of other
people's conceptions of himself and to embark upon an open psychological journey that enables him to achieve a new life as an emancipated man.
Unlike Beckett's narrator, he can see his life as a "road" that does make
"headway" because he sees himself as on the road to freedom.

Ishmael Reed's *Flight to Canada* likewise avoids the despair of experimental fiction such as *The Unnamable* because it aggressively disagrees
with narrators who complain that modern experience is so barren that it
does not permit us either to "discover" or "recover" meanings in life. Unlike Beckett's enervated persona who finds artistic creation a sterile dead
end because he can find "no words but the words of others," Raven Quickskill finds untapped linguistic resources available to him, both in terms of
his own verbal inventiveness and the rich resources of the black folk and
literary traditions. His story is much more than mere "lies" because it uses
language vitally to discover and recover meanings in African American
experience.

Flight to Canada, in the final analysis, does not use the picaresque
form reductively to drain it of meaning, envisioning life in entropic terms
as a "road" that disintegrates into incoherent movement and stasis. Rather,
it brilliantly revives the picaresque mode, imagining life as a new version
of the sort of open journey portrayed in a seminal American text such as
Adventures of Huckleberry Finn and a classic Afro-American text like
Narrative of the Life of Frederick Douglass. In this way, it adds new vitality to American and African American literary traditions, creating fresh
ways of portraying the open journey that have inspired subsequent black
writers.

7

Sherley Anne Williams's *Dessa Rose:*
Clearing Space in Time

Flight to Canada, in challenging and reversing the assumptions of enslaving texts like *Uncle Tom's Cabin*, seeks to liberate Afro-American fiction from the rigid stereotypes of black experience that have contributed to what Arnold Rampersad has characterized as a condition of "neoslavery"[1] in modern American life. Sherley Anne Williams's *Dessa Rose* takes this process much further, creating an Afro-American open journey in time, radically revising conventional visions of the slave past to clear a liberating space in Afro-American history and literary tradition. Her novel does this by elaborately deconstructing William Styron's *The Confessions of Nat Turner* (1968), a novel that envisions the slave past in hopelessly static terms, and then reconstructing a hopeful and dynamic vision of that past by echoing a wide range of nineteenth-century American texts that imagine the flight from slavery as an open journey.

Williams thus uses a literary strategy that Henry Louis Gates Jr. has called "signifyin[g]," a mode of discourse at the center of black American literary tradition that both repeats and artfully revises previous discourse, creating new meanings that are distinctively black. According to Gates, "signify[ing] is a uniquely black rhetorical concept, entirely textual or linguistic, by which a second figure repeats, or tropes, or reverses the first."[2] In this way, it can be a powerful source of intertextuality, a means by which a given text can enrich its meanings by repeating a pattern from an earlier text and then troping upon that pattern. For example, Ellison's *Invisible Man* echoes the central motifs of Washington's *Up from Slavery* and then ironically inverts them to produce a vision of black life that in many ways is the exact reverse of that contained in the earlier text. The signifying relationships between texts can also be celebratory, however, resulting in a book endowing itself with affirmative meanings from an earlier text. Alice

Walker's *The Color Purple*, for example, enriches its own vision by creatively echoing patterns from Hurston's *Their Eyes Were Watching God*. As Gates argues in *The Signifying Monkey*, signifying is a "formal revision" that can take the form of either "loving acts of bonding" between works with special affinities or "ritual slayings"[3] whereby a text subverts the meanings of another text and then displaces them with meanings of its own.

Dessa Rose brilliantly employs both types of signifying in order to envision the Afro-American past in fresh and liberating ways. The novel is clearly a "ritual slaying" of *The Confessions of Nat Turner*, a book that debunks a nineteenth-century black hero by reducing his narrative to the sort of purposeless wandering and paralysis depicted in postmodern novels such as Beckett's *The Unnamable* and Lowry's *Under the Volcano*. But it also deepens its vision by engaging in "loving acts of bonding" with other American texts that help the author to recover heroic significance from the slave past by imagining the flight from slavery as an open journey directed by will, imagination, and courage. Skillfully signifying upon books such as *Narrative of William Wells Brown, Running a Thousand Miles for Freedom,* and *Adventures of Huckleberry Finn*, Williams's novel conceives of time itself as a liberatingly open journey centered in human consciousness rather than a deterministic sequence shaped by environment.

In the "Author's Notes" that prefaces *Dessa Rose,* Williams reveals that as a child she "loved history" but felt that "there was no place in the American past where I could go and be free" because "literature and writing" about history had given her an essentially negative vision of the African American past. Novels like Styron's *The Confessions of Nat Turner*, for example, had "travestied" the oral memoirs of a nineteenth-century black hero, thus resulting in black readers being "betrayed" by a white account of the black past. Williams's reading of a study of slave revolts by black activist Angela Davis and historian Herbert Aptheker, however, opened up the black past for her, giving her glimpses of "that other history" characterized by "heroism and love" rather than victimhood. As a result, she was able to understand the past in a fundamentally creative way, producing the "invention" of her novel. It provided her with an affirmative vision that gave her a "metaphor" that allowed her to "own a summer in the 19th century." Aptheker's and Davis's texts, by signifying on standard accounts of the slave past, empowered her to create a new text, a "fiction" that is "based on fact."[4] Such a text provided her with a compellingly new view of time and history centered in freely willed acts that allow one to gain control over time, thus "owning" it. Through the creative process of her own reading and writing, Williams has emancipated herself from a static vision of history that robbed her of freedom and has committed herself instead to a dynamic vision of history as an open process inviting human growth.

Dessa Rose arises from a very similar process of signifying, first deconstructing *The Confessions of Nat Turner*, a book that strips the black past of meaning by envisioning it as a bleakly deterministic sequence. This can be vividly seen by contrasting the structures of the two novels. The narrative design of *The Confessions of Nat Turner* is clearly deterministic, beginning and ending with nearly identical stream of consciousness sequences that portray Nat's trapped, helplessly drifting consciousness slowly lapsing into Beckettian silence and inaction. Most of the novel's major scenes are brute repetitions of traumatic episodes that Nat never fully understands or controls—silently watching his mother being raped, witnessing Miss Emmeline's fornication, and compulsively murdering Margaret Whitehead. His agonized passivity in the first two scenes results in his erupting in mindless violence in the third scene; but in each scene Nat is portrayed as a helpless victim of powerful environmental determinants. Even when he plans a "divine mission" to liberate blacks, he succeeds only in achieving what Gray describes as "a flat-assed failure, a total fiasco" because Nat's revolt is rooted in a consciousness twisted by environment and characterized by religious fanaticism, repressed sexuality, self-hatred, and hatred of his fellow blacks. Nat is portrayed throughout the novel as a naturalistic victim of his own biology and forces from his social environment controlled by whites. He is finally seen as a person reduced to "an entombed, frustrated rage" whose narrative takes the form of an iron circle of necessity.[5]

Dessa Rose, however, reverses the structure of Styron's nihilistic text by dramatizing the central character's growing consciousness as she moves more freely in space, which becomes increasingly more open. Her narrative therefore is a linear progression from a condition of restriction to a state of freedom characterized by open movement in time. Dessa's story begins with her jailed in a cellar, a "dark hole" (48) that nearly reduces her to a condition of paralysis. But unlike Nat, who never successfully liberates himself in either a physical or psychological way, Dessa escapes to Sutton's Glen and eventually moves to the West to establish a new life for herself, her friends, and her family. This outward movement triggers steady human growth. Dessa begins the novel as a "barely visible" (9) person characterized by "halting speech and hesitant manner" (10) but becomes a heroic figure who can create a richly human identity for herself by "making a way out of no way," finding space in a world designed to deny space to blacks and then expanding and moving freely through this space. She thereby becomes what Styron's Nat Turner failed to become, an autonomous self engaged in acts that not only result in her own growth but also transform the social world and history. In all of these ways, she resembles the heroes and heroines of certain nineteenth-century American narratives dramatizing the flight from slavery—figures like Frederick Douglass, William Wells Brown, Harriet Jacobs, Mary Prince, and Huckleberry Finn, who could revolutionize their own lives and help transform history with their open journeys away from servitude to various kinds of freedom.

At many key points *Dessa Rose* consciously echoes classic slave narratives. For example, the novel's first chapter begins with a quote from Douglass's *Narrative*: "You have seen how a man was made a slave . . ." (8). Here the effect of signifying is double, since the first part of the sentence quoted from Douglass's book prepares us for the brutal way in which Dessa is immobilized in the opening chapter but the second part of Douglass's sentence which is not stated but strongly implied ("you shall see how a slave was made a man"),[6] suggests how Dessa has within her the same human resources that allow Douglass to rebel against slavery and forge a human identity by undertaking a heroic journey to freedom.

Dessa Rose also signifies upon two other important slave texts: *The Narrative of William Wells Brown* and *Running a Thousand Miles to Freedom, or the Escape of William and Ellen Craft from Slavery*. Ned's story of how he escaped punishment when his owner "sent him with a note down to the sheriff to be whipped" (228) echoes a story Brown tells in his narrative when he is sent on an identical errand. Brown subverts the intentions of his owner by having a white man first read the note to him so that he understands the instructions it contains and then he dupes another slave into delivering the note to the sheriff, who promptly administers the whipping. In this way he cleverly alters the journey he has been sent on, changing it from a set of movements directed by whites to motion that he controls with his own consciousness and will. Nat tells essentially the same story, but the effect is different. Whereas Brown gloats over his clever stratagem and waits around the corner "intending to see how my friend looked when he came out,"[7] Ned experiences a strong sense of remorse at having victimized a fellow black man and feels angry that the slave system had "made" (228) him perform such a cruel act. Whereas Brown amorally draws attention to his prowess as a trickster, Ned and his listeners indict slavery for forcing blacks to exploit each other in order to survive. Ned's story therefore evokes laughter, but it is very different from the unfeeling laughter of

Brown's narrative and stresses "We laughed so we wouldn't cry" (228). Ned's journey in the final analysis is different from Brown's journey—whereas Brown's movement to freedom is a highly individualistic effort to secure his own personal freedom, Ned sees his journey as part of a group effort designed to secure freedom not only for himself but for his fellow blacks as well.

The elaborate masquerade carried out by Dessa and her fellow slaves to secure their freedom invites strong comparison with the equally elaborate masquerade by William and Ellen Craft performed in 1848, a year after the fictional events of *Dessa Rose* take place. Ellen Craft, who was "almost white," disguised herself in male attire. She impersonated a sick male planter en route to Philadelphia for medical treatment who was accompanied by a black slave, a role that her husband William enacted. Several obvious plot similarities link Williams's novel with Craft's slave narrative—for example, the masqueraders do their planning at night while whites sleep, and they hide their money on the person playing the role of the slave, because whites assume that blacks are penniless. The Crafts also experience two crises that closely resemble the ordeal that Dessa undergoes in Arcopolis when Nehemiah recognizes her. While riding in a carriage in Richmond, William is claimed by an elderly white woman who identifies him as her "runaway nigger"; like Dessa, he gets through this crisis by calmly acting out the role of the subservient Negro before an audience of convinced whites. They pass a sterner test in Baltimore when Ellen is required by a white officer to provide proof of her ownership of William, either in the form of papers or security. Just as Nehemiah's words strike terror into Dessa's heart, the "sharp words" of the white officer trigger in William a deep fear of being returned to the "dark and horrible pit" of slavery. But his wife's skillful execution of the role of "invalid gentleman" saves the day in precisely the same way as Rufel's virtuoso performance in the role of "respectable white lady" rescues Dessa. At the crucial moment when the train leaves for Philadelphia, the officer relents in his demands, largely because he and other whites on the train car are so sympathetically disposed to what they perceive as a stricken gentleman and his faithful slave. By cleverly manipulating the sentimental stereotypes of a racist white audience, both the Crafts and the heroines of *Dessa Rose* are able to continue their journey to freedom.

The Crafts' narrative is useful to Williams in one other important way: it raises gender issues that are at the heart of *Dessa Rose*. The Crafts stress that slavery is particularly vicious toward black women because they can be exploited by "licentious monsters" who may buy a "virtuous and beautiful" black woman and then use her in any way they wish. Indeed, slave laws deny womanhood to slaves, reducing them to the level of "chattel." As William says of his wife, "The laws under which we lived did not recognize her as a woman." In a similar way, *Dessa Rose* defines a slave system that is not only racial in nature but is also premised upon gender dominations. As she comes to understand Dessa, Rufel realizes that both are enslaved by a social structure that treats women as things rather than people. And Dessa learns a similar lesson after she observes Rufel almost being raped by a drunken white man: "The white woman was subject to the same ravishment as me" (220). The journey in both works is therefore motivated by similar desires. The Crafts first go North and then to Europe for the same reason as Dessa and Harker head to the West—namely, to raise children in an environment free of racial and gender enslavement that destroys families.[8]

Related gender issues are probed in a scene late in *Dessa Rose* that signifies brilliantly upon the famous crisis of conscience episode in Twain's *Adventures of Huckleberry Finn*. Both novels are centered in picaresque journeys that bring white and black characters into intimate human contact with each other, ultimately producing powerful moral dilemmas that are a result of such contact. As Huck and Jim become more humanly real to each other, Huck's societally trained "conscience" conflicts sharply with the dictates of his heart—the former tells him that Jim is a piece of property that must be returned to its lawful owner while the latter prompts him to see Jim as a person and a friend to be freed from slavery. In the same way, Dessa's vision of Rufel is painfully split. Although her position in a racially divided society causes her to regard Rufel as a "white woman" who is a symbol of everything she "feared and hated" (182), her collaboration with Rufel on a journey to their mutual freedom enables her to see this woman in deeply human terms, as a friend and fellow victim of slavery. These two views of Rufel come into dramatic conflict late in the novel when Dessa contemplates Rufel's relationship with Nathan, a black man with whom Rufel wants to go to the West to establish a new life:

> She said some more, but I stopped listening at mention of Nathan. I hadn't thought that much about him and her living in a long time. Mostly, we had too much on our minds to be thinking about loving, least so far as everybody *act*. So it was easy to forget there was something more between them two. But now, when she said Nathan name, I membered setting up there on that wagon seat between them at the start of the journey. I could feel myself getting warm. "I thought you was going back to your peoples." I knowed she didn't set no store by her peoples, but that feeling of danger, of fear, was back. Couldn't she see what harm her being with Nathan would cause us? Hadn't her peoples taught her nothing? (238–39)

Like Twain, Williams does not sentimentalize the interrelationships between black and white people in America, because she stresses that even as
they grow in understanding and love for each other on one level of their
consciousness, on another level they remain apart, fearful of each other
and what their contact implies. Even though she has developed a friendship with Rufel that transcends the racist system each has grown up in,
another part of Dessa draws back from the "danger" created by this relationship and wants to abide by what white people ("Dessa's peoples") have
"taught" her—that the races are fundamentally different and should remain apart, especially in sexual matters. Similar societally induced "fear"
also convinces Huck that he and Jim should remain in separate worlds and
that he will go to "Hell" if he violates society's strictures by helping Jim to
secure his liberty.

When Rufel asks Dessa what she thinks of an interracial couple join-
ing them on their journey West, Dessa's unspoken fears quickly get verbal-
ized:

> "I think it scandalous, white woman chasing all around the country after
> some red-eyed Negro," I told her; and could've bit my tongue. She looked
> at me like I slapped her, face white as a sheet, them freckles standing out
> like hand-prints cross her jaw. "Speak, neither act out of turn"; seem like
> I could hear them words in my head. And it seem like I was bound to do
> one or the other. Oh, I had learned some on that journey. "Miss'ess," I
> say. And couldn't bring myself to say sorry; she'd risk us all for some
> belly rub. I mumbled something about it not being my place to speak. . . .
> (239)

Here the verbal echoes between Twain's and Williams's novels become
particularly clear and significant. Whenever Huck and Dessa use the language of official genteel culture, they express ideas that run counter to the
deeper human truths that they experience on the nonrational levels of their
beings. The "words" in Dessa's "head" are like the "words" Huck tries to
summon up as he tries to put an "idea" down on a note to his master that
would result in Jim being sent back to slavery. When Huck views Jim
through the prism of official language that he gets from "Sunday school,"
he sees a "nigger," not a man, and thus feels burdened by his own "wicked-
ness" for helping Jim escape.[9] In a similar way, when Dessa employs words
like "scandalous" she can visualize Rufel only in the stereotypes that her
culture makes available to her, as a "white woman" interested in forbidden
sex (a "belly rub") with an equally stereotyped "red-eyed Negro." Her language reduces a loving relationship between a man and a woman to a

trivialized relationship between two stereotypical figures acting out the fantasies of a racially divided culture. When Dessa, as Huck is often inclined to do, summons up scripture ("Speak, neither act out of turn") she likewise separates herself from the troubling relationships that Rufel reminds her of. This separation destroys the human intimacy that has been established between them; left in its place is a safer but sterile relationship in which each woman occupies their own "place" in a segregated society.

Both scenes conclude in similar ways. Huck's deepest level of moral imagination asserts itself when he impulsively rips up the note he had planned to send to Miss Watson. Dessa's deepest moral promptings are likewise jarred into action when she loudly slams an object against the door after Rufel leaves the room in anger. At this point, Dessa's socially conditioned consciousness that distances her from Rufel gives way to the human feelings welling up from her subconsciousness, which seek human contact with Rufel:

> . . . and I heard something thud against the door. I stood there in the hall
> breathing fast, wanting things back like they was when we come in from
> lunch, her Miz Lady and me the one she was partnered with in the scheme,
> wishing she'd come to the door and say what she'd said again. (240)

Dessa now welcomes the words that Rufel shouts before slamming the door: "Well, I ain't talking no 'place' . . . I'm talking friends" (239). Like Huck, who heroically commits himself to a human relationship with Jim despite the severe penalties he will pay for this commitment, Dessa ultimately accepts the dangers of her sisterhood with Rufel, whom she finally calls by her real name "Ruth," revealing that she no longer sees her as a "mistress" (255) but has become her friend and sister.

Rufel's freeing of Dessa from the Arcopolis jail might also be viewed as signifying on Tom and Huck attempting to free Jim from imprisonment on the Phelps plantations. In both cases, elaborate masquerades are used to confuse white people who endanger the freedom of a black central character, but the nature of each masquerade is quite different. As Judith Fetterly has observed, the games that Tom plays with Jim are motivated by "cruelty"[10] and are rooted in a kind of "madness" that perversely endangers Jim's life rather than liberating him from slavery. But unlike Tom, who uses his powers as a "fictionist" to amorally manipulate people, Rufel uses her imagination in a pragmatic and moral way to free Dessa. Then too, Tom's "farcical inventions," as Leo Marx has pointed out, reduce Jim to a "flat stereotype" that divests him of "much of his dignity and individuality."[11] But Dessa only acts out a stereotyped role in Rufel's masquerade, always clearly aware of the difference between her own humanity and the role she has to play in this particular situation to protect her humanity.

However much Williams revises Twain's novel, she remains in strong agreement with Twain on one crucial point. The racial dilemmas of the United States are too complex and too embedded in a problematic history to be easily resolved. Both writers do not let us forget that their black and white central characters separate at the end of their respective journeys, never to see each other again. Although Williams and Twain envision the West as a freer space than the pre–Civil War American South, neither is willing to make the West a utopia that can magically resolve American racial problems, or any other human problems, for that matter. Huck lights out to the territories, which may or may not provide him with a new life, while Jim simply disappears. Dessa and Harker go West, even though they have been told that the "West was closed to the black" (258), because they realize that even though such a land "set us a hard task" (259), the courage and resourcefulness that have freed them from southern slavery can give them and their descendents better lives in a new country. The evidence supplied in the novel's epilogue clearly indicates that they have succeeded, establishing families, a community, and a vitalizing tradition that they not only "wrote down" but that their children "say back" (260).

Ruth, like Jim, vanishes, going vaguely East to what Dessa describes as "some city [that] didn't allow no slaves" (258). Here Williams signifies on Twain's novel with a revealing difference—it is her black characters who move to what in American literature has been traditionally defined as an area of renewal and expanded possibility, using such space to establish "our children's place in the world" (260). In sharp contrast, Williams's white heroine can only disappear, finally becoming the sort of ambiguous question mark that Jim is in Twain's novel.

Williams therefore uses texts such as *Adventures of Huckleberry Finn,* *Narrative of the Life of Frederick Douglass, Running a Thousand Miles for Freedom,* and *The Narrative of William Wells Brown* as lenses through which she can view the slave past as a liberating vision, transforming it from the bleakly deterministic sequence of events imagined in novels such as *The Confessions of Nat Turner.* Her central character, Dessa Rose, must also overcome a deterministic sense of time that enslaves her and reduces her to the level of a thing; she must experience time as an open journey that enables her to actualize her human potential. At the beginning of the novel

Dessa is not only physically trapped in a cellar that is described as a "dark hole" (48) and has been subjected to the torture of being placed in a "sweatbox" (142) that nearly kills her; she is also trapped in time, psychologically paralyzed by a traumatic past that deprives her of a future and drains her present experiences of meaning. Sentenced to death but forced to await execution for several months until her baby is born, she is also psychologically numbed by the violent death of her lover Kaine, who was killed when he attacked his master:

> Memory stopped the day Emmalina met her as she had come out of the fields. Dessa came back to that moment again and again, recognizing it as dead, knowing there was no way to change it, arriving at it from various directions, refusing to move beyond it. Out there was nightmare, Kaine's body, cold and clammy beneath her hands, Master laughing in her face, the horror that scarred her inner thighs, snaking around her lower abdomen and hips in ropy keloids that gleamed with patent-leather smoothness. Once the white man's questioning had driven her into that desert and young Mistress had risen from the waste, clothes torn, hair screaming, red-faced, red mouthed. . . . She had seen the blood and bits of pink flesh beneath her own fingernails, felt again the loose skin of Young Mistress's neck. And clamped her mouth shut, clanked her arms across her chest. She should have killed the white woman; they would have killed her then. It would have been all over; none of this would have begun. (56–57)

Psychologically and emotionally frozen by this dead moment, Dessa wishes that she had killed her mistress so that her own life would be "all over" and she could be released from the flow of time. Condemned to live in a sterile present as she awaits her execution, she, like Bigger Thomas, alternates between rage and apathy, both of which exhaust her and make significant movement impossible. She listlessly "mark[s] time" (58) as she mechanically submits to being interviewed by Nehemiah, while secretly burning with hatred towards all whites. Her mind "numbed," she regards the past as "sealed" (58) because it has culminated in a moment that has destroyed her reason for living and she is unable to "move beyond" such a moment. The past therefore has become a "desert," a "waste" that has robbed her of vitality and infused her with a suicidal drive that closely resembles the self-destructive compulsions of Styron's Nat Turner. Like Nat she later feels "buried under years of silence" (126) and sees herself as "wallowing in what had hurt" (186) her.

Unlike Nat, who never overcomes the debilitating effects of his traumatic past and who therefore is driven on by past events that deplete his present of meaning and destroy his future, Dessa has within her human resources that enable her to overcome her entrapment in time. Although her memory is locked in a "dead" moment in the past, her imagination can bring her to a point prior to this when she and Kaine enjoyed a vital present that moved into an open future. As she sleeps in the cellar that functions as her jail, she dreams of Kaine, picturing him with images of free movement. His voice is described as "clear as running water" as he is "striding" (1) to meet her. She is described as "running, running" (2) to him as his fingers snap in a "rhythm" that is the "same one that powered her heart" (1–2). This entire scene is perceived in terms of graceful, lively movement—"children ran here and there" while the Quarters "stirred" and smoke "curled lazily from several stovepipes" (2). Feeling the "steady beat of his heart against her own" (4), she becomes part of a vital world "suffused" by "love" (3) which is always moving and growing.

Henry Louis Gates Jr., in a discussion of Douglass's *Narrative,* has observed that, for a slave, memory was crucial for self-definition, because the slave lived in a world where written documents either ignored blacks or misrepresented them. Lacking the written documents that would record the slave's birth date and other crucial events, the slave virtually became a "prisoner" of memory:

> In antebellum America, it was the deprivation of time in the life of the slave that first signaled his or her status as a piece of property. Slavery's time was delineated by memory and memory alone. One's sense of one's existence, therefore, depended upon memory. It was memory, above all, that gave shape to being itself. . . . For the dependence upon memory made the slave, first and foremost, a slave to himself or herself, a prisoner of his or her own power of recall.[12]

When Dessa Rose's memory is crippled by a traumatic event in the past, therefore, her very self is at risk, in danger of dying. But whereas her memory brings her toward death (recall of Kaine's death literally results in a desire for her own death), her imagination keeps her alive by enlivening her consciousness with powerful images of love and movement. Even though she was outwardly immobilized in her cell as she "lay listlessly on the pallet or sat against a wall" (53), her "mind continued to roam" (54) as she imagined "dreams that crowded around her in the cellar" but "now walked in the sunlit air" (56). The songs she sings also stimulate her imagination, providing her with hopeful images of movement and new life. As she is being interviewed for a book Nehemiah is writing that will help whites to quell slave revolts and fix her in the stereotyped role of "darky," she sings

"Lawd, give me wings like Noah's dove" (31). Later she sings "Gonna march away in the gold band / In the army by and by" (48), a verse that Nehemiah dismisses as a "quaint piece of doggerel" (49) but that inspires in her faint hopes of escape. Indeed, her eventual escape is in part orchestrated by a call-response song which she sings with the slaves. They use the song to coordinate their movements and communicate their intents. Significantly, the song itself is filled with images of free movement:

> Soul's going to heaven
> Soul's going to ride that heavenly train
> Cause the Lawd have called you home.
>
> (64)

These images of movement which have kept Dessa from despair are now replaced by physical movement that brings her to a new life. As she begins her escape, her child moves vigorously in her womb and is born the next day when she is on the road to freedom. Putting herself in open motion, "She had lost track of place, and time" (89) and begins to see both in new ways. Time is no longer a dead zone in which she awaits execution but is a vital process that gives her the possibility of moving in the present toward a liberating future. Likewise, she no longer feels trapped by place. Whereas her previous life was riveted to a "permanent place" (55), a geographically confined area that robbed her of individuality by enslaving her with restrictive social roles and mind-numbing work, she now moves meaningfully toward open space for the first time in her life. The room she has in Rufel's house is a "spacious and light-filled chamber" (96), a sharp contrast to the other confining rooms in which she has lived her previous life. Moreover, Rufel's plantation is physically isolated, an "undeveloped . . . sparse settlement" (107) that is unusually free of many of the restrictions of southern society. The master of Sutton's Glen has abandoned the place and Rufel allows slaves to be on almost an equal footing with her; blacks and whites share roles. (Indeed, Rufel serves as a wet nurse to Dessa's baby, forms a romantic relationship with a black man, and eventually becomes close friends with a group of escaped slaves, assisting them in their escape from racial slavery as they assist her in an escape from gender slavery.)

The masquerade they perform as they travel through central Alabama to secure the money they need to go West further frees them from the enslaving roles of southern culture because, in parodying the roles of slave and master, they psychologically free themselves of these roles and the racist assumptions underpinning them. Whereas Dessa characterizes her earlier life as "belong[ing] to a place" and "not mov[ing] too far from it" (195), she and her friends now move freely through a variety of southern places, mastering them with a brilliant con game that provides them with the money they need. Harker animates their movements with his nearly mythic image of the West as a free space offering a new life:

> And Harker got us all fired up about the West. He could put some words together, make you see broad, grassy valleys, clear, sparkling streams, a river that divided slave land from free. (182)

Although they eventually discover that the actual West is a much harsher place than this mythic West because it is surely not altogether free of racism and is in some respects "closed to the black" (258), Dessa and her group do establish a new life on the frontier. At the end of the novel she admits that the new "country have set us a hard task" (259), but she remains convinced of her earlier belief that "The West had to be better than here" (184), the enslaved world of the South. And the evidence provided at the end of the novel clearly justifies her optimism. She, her family, and her friends finally do reach a new space that enables them to "own ourselfs" (260), establishing a fruitful new life in which they prosper as a family and secure their "children's place in the world" (260). The nameless western spot in which they settle is not without a "cost" (260), but it does function for them as the frontier functioned for traditional American heroes and heroines, as a redemptive new land offering new growth, limitless possibilities.

The growth that Dessa achieves in her open journeys results in her experiencing time as a dynamic flux containing new possibilities, thus freeing her from the temporal entrapment that threatened her with death in the opening parts of the novel. This growth is accelerated and deepened as she forms human relationships in her journey. In her relationship with Harker, for example, she overcomes the emotional impasse she reached as a result of Kaine's death. Like Kaine, who is persistently associated with free movement, Harker is a "wanderer" (156), a picaresque figure who has managed to achieve an unusual degree of freedom in the slave South. He is also perceived by Dessa as "thunder and lightning" (209) that shakes Dessa from her psychological and physical lethargy, assisting her in her escape from slavery and helping her to heal the wounds she has received from the slave system. When he proposes marriage to Dessa, therefore, she immediately links her relationship with Harker to her rebirth in time:

> I had him a long time by then; not in years, no. I had known him only weeks. But he had brought me out of that cellar, had birthed my baby and

sat beside me while I laid in that bed. We talked and I felt I had knowed him deep. And here he was promising himself to me, talking about a future he wanted for us, and this frightened me. Kaine hadn't done this. You know, the future did not belong to us; it belonged to our masters. We wasn't to think about no future; it was a sign of hellaciousness if we did. (209–10)

Her relationship with Harker broadens and deepens Dessa's sense of time, releasing her from a deterministic past and making the present an occasion for freely willed action that gives her a belief in the future. This sense of time as a continuum centered in human consciousness and will helps her to see the future as something that "belongs" to her, because she can shape it to meet her own needs to ensure her own growth.

The relationship she develops with Rufel also contributes to growth that brings her beyond the temporal paralysis afflicting her at the beginning of the novel. At the moment Kaine was murdered, Dessa had "become a self she scarcely knew, lost to family and to friends" (56). In her rage she attempts to strangle her mistress and is fixed in a hatred of white people that deadens her emotionally and locks her in a moment of regret over not having acted effectively on her murderous impulses. Williams makes it clear here that Dessa's feelings here are understandable but debilitating, for they freeze her in a stance that is suicidal. Dessa's desire to kill her mistress is tied in with a more fundamental desire to obliterate herself—for to perform this act would immediately bring on her own death at the hands of her masters. Just as her assault on her mistress produces a terrible whipping that scars her body, it also results in her being inwardly "crippled" (208). However, her slowly developing relationship with Rufel heals Dessa of many of the wounds she has received as a slave, thus enabling her to move forward in time. Just as Harker serves to physically free her and deliver her baby, Rufel helps to emotionally free her of the sort of rage that consumes Styron's Nat Turner when she breast-feeds Dessa's baby. Although she initially resents Rufel's nursing of Mony, she comes to see this act of spontaneous love as redemptive:

We stayed that night at the plantation of Mr. Oscar; Nathan was sent round to the Quarters with the rest of our people but I stayed with Miz Lady. This is where I began another part of my education. When I come to myself in that bed, I accepted that everyone I loved was gone. That life was dead to me; I'd held the wake for it in that cellar. Yet and still, I was alive. At first I couldn't put no dependence on what I was seeing—a *white* woman nursing a *negro*; negroes acting good as *free*. *I* wasn't even posed to be there. I didn't make no sense of what I was seeing, much less what

I'd been doing. I was someone I knowed and didn't know, living in a world I hadn't even knowed was out there. So that bed was a grave and a birthing place to me. (214–15)

The bed she shares with Rufel and their children serves as a metaphor of their deepening relationship, which helps Dessa to overcome the temporal entrapment symbolized by the tomblike "cellar" and to nurture a new self that is both "alive" and "free." When she heard about Kaine's death, she had "become a self she scarcely knew, lost to family, to friends" (56) but now she becomes yet another self, "someone I knowed and didn't know, living in a world I hadn't even knowed was out there." Such a world not only leads to her recovery of family and friends in the form of Mony, Harker, Rufel, and all the others who join her on their journey West, but it also helps her come to a hopeful vision of time as ongoing movement to an indeterminate future. The bed that she shares with Rufel and their children therefore is a "grave" in the sense that it destroys a nightmare past that threatens her growth; but it is also a "birthing place" that gives her a new identity and a new way of positioning herself in the flow of time.

By the end of the novel Dessa sees time in Bergsonian terms as continuous flow, as past spills into a dynamic present and the two move on to a future that is always growing. Seen in these terms, her past with Kaine has not resulted in her physical and psychic death but a new life, their baby. The present is no longer an empty space where she merely "marks time" but an invitation to creation, action that produces new possibilities. And the future is open, not closed; it no longer belongs to one's masters but to one's self and one's community.

This vision of time as an organic continuum, an open journey generating limitless growth, is vividly dramatized at the beginning and ending of the novel. In her "Author's Note" Williams explains that she was able to overcome a deterministic vision of the past in which she could not be "free" (x) when she rejected books like Styron's *Confessions* and wrote her own novel about the slave past that was centered in "heroism" and "love" (x). No longer "at the mercy of literature and writing" (ix) that have "betrayed" (xi) black people by racist interpretations of Afro-American history that portray blacks as passive victims, she can now "own a summer in the 19th century" (x). Instead of limiting her, the past is transfigured, inspiring her to shape the present creatively in order to achieve a more humane future. In a very similar way, Dessa Rose gains control over time and becomes whole in time when she not only escapes from slavery to freedom but also *writes* her story for posterity, thus keeping alive in the reader's consciousness the crucial idea that the past is not a deterministic force imposing its designs on the present and closing off the future but is part of an organic continuum shaped by will and imagination. When Dessa's oral and written discourse make the past available to her son, he internalizes it, "know[ing] it by heart" and then "tell[ing] it to his babies like the memories was his" (259). This handing over of a living past to the present is not a regressive, nostalgic act bringing people backwards in time; rather, it is a vitally prospective act urging people to go forward in time. For Dessa's story is a challenge to future generations to continue the struggle against the forms of slavery persisting in their own times. Because Dessa is not content merely to record her story, to "have it wrote down," she insists that the children "say it back" (260), establishing a vital continuity between past and present that urges people to *use* the struggles of the past to continually expand possibilities in the future.

Thus enclosed by scenes that envision time as an open journey driven by human will and imagination, *Dessa Rose* celebrates black history from slavery to the present. In so doing, Williams's novel creates important new space in Afro-American history and literary tradition.

Williams's novel provides strong evidence against the argument made in recent years that American journey literature is an exclusively male genre that cuts against the grain of women's values. Elizabeth Ammons, for example, has argued that the tradition of American women's literature sharply diverges from writing by American males because it centers itself in "matrifocal" values that stress "group salvation" in domesticated places rather than individual salvation achieved by an isolated hero moving away from the social world toward open space. In her analysis of *Uncle Tom's Cabin* she states:

> My thesis throughout is that Stowe's manipulation of maternal ideology is adapted and remodelled in illuminating ways in the work of American women writers before the 1920s and that, taken together, this body of fiction from Stowe forward constitutes a rich female tradition in American literature that challenges the dominant, twentieth-century, academic construction of the canon in terms of the adventure tale and the antisocial, which is to say antifeminine, escape narrative. Stated simply: in the tradition that Stowe heads, if we look at it simply and on its own terms, there exists an important and radical challenge to the emerging industrial-based definition of community as something organized by work,

ruled by men and measured by productivity of things. . . . In place of that
ideal there is posited by a number of women writers, black and white, an
alternative matrifocal concept: an ideal of community as something defined by family (rather than work), measured by relationships (rather than
products) and ruled by women (rather than men). It is a vision of community at least as radical as the more frequently valorized indictment of
American culture offered by nineteenth-century male writers, who, one
could argue, simply fled, taking to the sea or a raft, or a shed by a pond—
seeking in solitude or at most couplehood (Huck and Jim; Ishmael and
Queequeg), individual salvation. Women writers in the nineteenth century, in contrast, can more often be seen seeking group salvation. Characteristically, they do not look for escape *from* society, but escape into some
recovered or reconstituted social system more humane and nonviolent
than that of Victorian America.[13]

Susan Gilbert and Sandra Gubar in *The Madwoman in the Attic* make a
similar point, arguing that certain genres, especially those depicting social
mobility and adventure in the outward world, are "essentially male" in
their outlook:

> From the rake-rogue to his modern counterpart, the traveling salesman,
> moreover, our comic heroes are quintessentially male in their escapades
> and conquests, while from the epic to the historical novel, the detective
> story to the "Western," European and American narrative literature has
> concentrated much of its attention on male characters who occupy public
> roles from which women have always been excluded.

As a result of either being excluded from or "locked into male texts" that
did not allow them to tell their stories, much women's literature is characterized by what Gilbert and Gubar call "agoraphobia," a literature of domestic enclosure in which trapped women like the central character of "The
Yellow Wallpaper" eventually "develop pathological fears of public places
and unconfined spaces."[14]

Journey books written by Afro-American women call these generalizations into sharp question. Black women such as Ellen Craft and Harriet
Jacobs who escaped slavery certainly rejected the enclosed places that symbolized their condition as slaves and did not shrink from exploring "unconfined spaces," thus liberating themselves and their families by undertaking
open journeys. Janie Crawford, the heroine of *Their Eyes Were Watching
God*, journeys to the open spaces of the Florida Everglades, which transform her consciousness and commit her to seeking a new "horizon" in her
"soul" (159) even when she is outwardly confined by the end of her novel.

Toni Morrison's fiction centers on heroines who have two equally liberating options: one, encompassing what Ammons calls "individual salvation," is achieved by open journeying; the other, "group salvation," is achieved by settling into a community of friends and family. Alice Walker's *Meridian*, likewise, presents its central character's open journey in complexly double terms, both as a personal quest for individual freedom and a political quest for a renewed black society.

Williams's *Dessa Rose* is clearly what Ammons calls an "escape narrative," dealing as it does with a number of people setting out on a journey to escape several kinds of slavery, but it is in no way "antifeminine" or "antisocial." The journey depicted in Williams's novel, like so many important texts written by Afro-American women, does not dichotomize personal and group freedom; rather, it views them as complementary functions of each other. While Dessa's epic journey certainly does liberate individuals from a society that reduces them to the status of things deprived of personhood, it does not become antisocial—that is, at variance with what Ammons terms "an ideal of community." Quite to the contrary, it stresses that genuine communities are made up of strong individuals who are not subsumed by their social roles and that humanly satisfying communities are not restrictive places but social spaces that allow for personal growth, social change, and a developing group identity. Although the journey portrayed in *Dessa Rose* is not centered in the kind of selfish individualism that expresses itself in Bertie Sutton's desertion of his family, neither is it sentimentally centered in what Ammons calls "motherhood." Instead, the journey accommodates both individual and communal needs as a variety of people move to create a society that is both fluid enough to allow individuals to grow and firm enough to give them a common identity.

Williams's novel, therefore, does not simply reject traditional literary forms such as the escape narrative and the picaresque novel but assimilates them, adapting them for new purposes. In this way it is squarely in line with the main tradition of Afro-American literature, which has characteristically modified and even transformed American art forms to express new black meanings. Such a literary tradition, as Gates reminds us, signifies "with a black difference."[15] Sherley Anne Williams, like the many African American writers she joins in an always growing tradition, puts new wine into old (but very useful) bottles, thus creating an important variation in the tradition of black American journey literature.

8

Twenty-First-Century Journeys in Octavia E. Butler's *Parable of the Sower*

I am not going to spend my life as some kind of twenty-first-century slave.

So we became the crew of a modern underground railroad.
                                            —*Parable of the Sower*

Octavia E. Butler's fiction takes the African American journey motif one step further by projecting it quite literally into the future. Eight of her ten published novels are set in futuristic societies in which her heroic figures cope with and transcend various kinds of entrapment by undertaking an interesting assortment of open journeys.

Patternmaster (1976) describes a society that is controlled by an all-powerful ruler who dominates the inward and outward lives of his subjects by ruthlessly imposing a "pattern" of thought and behavior on them. Teray and Amber, the novel's dual heroes, seek to break away from this form of "physical slavery" and "mental slavery" by setting themselves in open motion. Amber, who is presented as an "independent" woman who is a "houseless wanderer," helps Teray overcome the tyranny of his brother Coransee by entering a liberating world of free space and motion. After killing Coransee, he breaks free of the "patterns" that have crippled him and he is able to experience physical and psychological freedom that is described in terms of open motion:

The canopy of awareness first seemed almost as broad as the sky itself.

Feeling like some huge bird, he projected his awareness over the territory. He could see, could sense, the lightly wooded land dotted with ruined buildings. He could see the distant ranges of hills, was aware of

133

the even-more-distant mountains. The mountains were far beyond his striking range. In fact they were near Forsyth, still over a day's journey away, but he could see them. He swooped about, letting his extended awareness range free through the hills and valleys.[1]

All of Butler's patternist novels are centered in this quest to transcend the mental structures and social institutions that imprison people in roles defined by hierarchical societies that are essentially feudal in character. Anyanwu, the heroine of *Wild Seed*, escapes various forms of slavery in Africa and America by becoming a fugitive in search of free space. A "shapeshifter" who can, like the Greek god Proteus, always change her outward forms to escape the entrapments that authority figures design for her, she becomes at several points in the novel a bird flying away from danger or a dolphin who can be "cleansed" by swimming in the sea. Like Ellison's invisible man, her identity is essentially fluid and indeterminate, always moving to new stages of development. Her antagonist Doro, however, has a rigidly fixed personality and is described as "a tortoise encased in a shell that gets thicker and thicker each year."[2] Whereas Anyanwu's function in the novel is to free herself and others from oppressive ideas and social structures, Doro is intent on building slave communities in Africa and America that give him absolute power over his subjects.

Imago (1989), likewise, presents two worlds in conflict, a "hierarchical" society that freezes people into static roles and a free society of Onkali, "space-going people" who envision life as a dynamic process of discovery and growth. While human beings dominate each other and kill those who do not fit into the "patterns" that they have constructed, the Onkali are engaged in an ongoing quest, a "long, long search for new species to combine with to construct new life forms." Fully intending "to leave the solar system in perhaps three centuries," they envision life as a colossal open journey, an ongoing search for fresh space providing new life.[3]

Butler's fiction, therefore, clears new space for African American literature by using a science fiction mode in which black writers have rarely shown interest and infusing this mode with social and political themes that are relevant to contemporary black people. But her work is also in the main tradition of black American literature dating back to the slave narratives. In a 1984 interview with Margaret O'Connor she pointed out that much of her fiction was inspired by "the narratives of Frederick Douglass and others who endured slavery."[4] Indeed, most of her work can be seen as signifying powerfully on the slave narratives, projecting them into the future and probing the residual effects of pre–Civil War slavery in present day and future America. Like the authors of nineteenth-century slave narratives, Butler envisions freedom as a radically open journey that must be experienced on physical, mental, and spiritual levels.

Parable of the Sower, published in 1993, is an appropriate book with which to conclude this study of the African American journey motif, because it not only imagines the open journey in fresh ways but it also signifies meaningfully on every major text examined in this study. The social world envisioned in the novel clearly echoes the nightmarish city depicted in *Native Son*, a deadening place of walled neighborhoods that trap the masses and walled estates that protect the rich from the misery they have created. Lauren Olamina, the novel's central character, describes her community of Robledo in terms that are strikingly similar to the way Bigger Thomas perceives the ghetto that threatens him. As she travels through her neighborhood she observes that

> A lot of our ride was along one neighborhood wall after another; some a block long, some two blocks, some five. . . . Up toward the hills there were walled estates—one big house and a lot of shaky little dependencies where the servants lived. . . . In fact we passed a couple of neighborhoods so poor that their walls were made up of unmortared rocks, chunks of concrete, and trash. Then there were the pitiful, unwalled residential areas. A lot of the houses were trashed—burned, vandalized, infested with drunks or druggies or squatted in by homeless families with their filthy, gaunt, half-naked children.[5]

In such a "dangerous" and "crazy" place people are reduced to the same "fear and hate" (31) that afflict everyone in *Native Son*. Physical movement is so dangerous that very few people dare to venture out of their walled communities and, when they do, they are either murdered like Lauren's father, tortured like her brother, or raped like the four-year-old girl to whom Lauren has become a surrogate sister. Social mobility has been destroyed by a devastated economy and intellectual growth has been stamped out by the complete elimination of any systems of education. Robledo becomes a frightening metaphor of America in gridlock, a world that closely resembles the nineteenth-century plantation that trapped Frederick Douglass and the twentieth-century ghetto that immobilized Bigger Thomas. But America in the twenty-first century is even worse than it was in the past, for slavery has been universalized to include all ethnic and racial groups in all regions of the country. All America has become a massive plantation, a gigantic ghetto.

Like Ralph Ellison and Charles Johnson, who sometimes portray the city as a Dantean underworld, Butler depicts an urban society that has "gone to hell" (257) and is "teetering on the abyss" (59). Butler's America has degenerated to such a point that it is seen in apocalyptic terms as a new version of "Jericho" (48) and "Babylon" (128), a culture that is paralyzed and on the verge of collapsing under the weight of its own corruption. Like Ishmael Reed, Butler envisions America in the first quarter of the twenty-first century as having returned to a condition of "slavery" in which "the country has slipped back 200 years" (274).

But *Parable of the Sower*, like the vast majority of classic African American journey books, does not present a vision of apocalyptic despair or an enervating nihilism. The heroine of the novel can save herself and others by constructing "a modern underground railroad" (262) taking them north to liberating new spaces. Such spaces not only take the form of an actual "sanctuary" (284) in the external world but also become mental, spiritual, and moral frontiers within the self. For Butler envisions the self as most African American picaresque writers do, as a protean process of limitless becoming rather than a completed state of being rooted in a particular place. Her heroine therefore is in a direct line of descent from Hurston's Janie Crawford, Walker's Ruth Copeland, Morrison's Pilate, and Williams's Dessa Rose, since all of these heroines transcend social roles that "place" them in restrictive identities by experiencing open journeys toward social freedom and personal transformation.

Lauren Olamina's central task is to find a way of moving from such constricting places to liberating spaces. Early in the novel she fears that "there are no safe places to move" (47). Her own small city of Robledo is "a dying and backward place" (122) where nearly all social institutions and moral values have collapsed and, as a result, a sense of community has been destroyed, reducing people to a bleakly Darwinian struggle for existence in a jungle of selfishness and violence. Feral dogs roam freely in the streets, which are populated mainly by "the street poor" (9). Drug-maddened "crazies" (98) burn down the few vestiges of civilization such as churches and makeshift homes while police and firemen refuse to do their jobs without extra payment, which very few citizens can afford. Things get worse when one moves beyond Robledo to places such as Los Angeles, which is described as a "carcass which is filled with maggots" (8), or southern Mississippi and Louisiana, which are experiencing cholera epidemics caused by a hopelessly polluted water supply. A new community in a suburb of Los Angeles called Olivar offers an equally dim prospect. A town that has been "bought and privatized" by a gigantic multinational corporation intent on reducing its citizens to the "debt slavery" (107) found in early-twentieth-century company towns, Olivar is an even "bigger dead-end" (125) than Robledo.

The novel's opening scene clearly dramatizes Lauren's desire to escape from such a trap. The book begins with her describing a "recurring dream" that she has whenever she feels confined, "twist[ing] on [her] own personal hook" (3). She pictures her neighborhood as a "crouching animal" that is "more threatening than protective" and then imagines herself as in a room whose walls are "burning" (4). In sharp contrast with these grim images of paralysis and death are hopeful images of open motion and space. She envisions herself as "learning to fly" or "levitate" (4) and, as the fire spreads through the room that threatens to become her coffin, she flies through a "door" (4) which brings her into open space illuminated by "cool pale, glinting light" (4) that allows her to look up at "the broad sweep of the Milky Way" (5). Her vision is further clarified and enriched when she comes to see the stars as not only "free" but "windows into heaven. Windows for God to look through and keep an eye on us" (5).

The entire novel is telescoped in this remarkable opening scene because it clearly equates place with death and open movement in free space with a new life. Lauren's physical journey begins after her family and home have been destroyed by several acts of senseless violence. Her old life gone, she does what most American and African American picaros do in such situations—she instinctively lights out for new frontiers, "heading North" (73) into what she hopes will be a "better life" (77). Like Frederick Douglass, she sees the North as an indeterminate space rather than a definite place. She knows that actual places such as Oregon are "closed" (73) because its citizens are deeply afraid of the refugees who might settle there and thus cause additional economic and social problems. Armed with a backpack containing only her journals, poems, and seed, she sets herself in quintessentially American pure motion, desiring only to "just run and run" (141). She knows exactly what she is leaving but has only the vaguest notion of where she is heading. As she joins the "river of people" (137) who have become fugitives in their own land, she asks herself, "Where were the westward walkers going?" (139) Her very American answer is "To something . . ." (157).

Her physical travels bring her to progressively larger and freer forms of open space, which offer her relief from a social world that is literally "falling apart" (247) from massive earthquakes and morally disintegrating from sociopathic behavior. She avoids cities that have been overrun by scavengers, cops, private security guards, druggies, and other "predators" intent on "destroying what's left" (221). When she and her growing group of companions reach the Pacific Ocean, an enormous open space that is described as "half a world of water" (189), they begin to sense a better life. Psychologically and physically refreshed by the water that cleanses them and the sheer space that fires their imaginations, they notice that the many people camping on the beach have also been "lulled" (184) by the ocean into less violent, more humane behavior. They later reach an area outside of Sacramento that they marvel at, "rich country" that has not been affected either by earthquakes or human violence, a world that offers them "more water, more food, more room . . . " (264). After Taylor Bankole joins them, they direct themselves toward the "safe haven" (244) of his three hundred acres of farmland in northern California, a "godsend" (246) that offers them a "better life" (228) by giving them a sanctuary from the bondage of the past.

This outward movement triggers inward journeys that are psychological, spiritual, and moral in character. As their external surroundings become more spacious, their inward selves deepen and mature. Although Lauren has just turned eighteen when her voyage begins, she soon realizes that her experiences on the road have made her a "woman" and not just a "kid" (209). No longer is she imprisoned by the "walls" of her own life; she now can break free of all restrictions that have held her back in the past and shape a radically new self. As she stresses in a poem she writes late in the novel:

> The self must create
> its own reasons for being.
> To shape God.
> Shape self.
>
> (291)

Implicit in Lauren's dynamic view of the self as a process that is always developing is a religious vision that is clearly nonteleological, a theology that regards God and the universe as always changing, always evolving. Lauren emphatically rejects the static views of God that she has received from her Baptist upbringing. She moves away from her father's "fortress church" (12), which is surrounded by walls and protected by armed guards and barbed wire, because such a church is grounded in rigid dogma and narrow morality that stifles her spirit. In a larger sense, she rejects traditional notions of God as a "big-daddy-God or a big-cop-God or a big-king-God" (13), because such stale concepts reduce God to an unchanging place in "nature" (13), making him an authority enforcing the mechanical rules of a hierarchical society that oppresses people.

She comes to see God as pure process, a dynamic life force that is always changing:

> . . . God is Pliable
> Trickster,
> Teacher,
> Chaos,
> Clay.
> God exists to be shaped.
> God is Change.
>
>   (22)

This sense of God leads her eventually to develop a new religion called Earthseed, a free and open religion that reflects the dynamic, protean nature of the soul and God. Rather than imagine her religion in conventional terms as a church with "walls" and a solid "foundation," she pictures it in terms of open motion, as seeds that are

> . . . windborne, animalborne, waterborne, far from their parent plants. They have no ability at all to travel great distances under their own power, and yet, they do travel. Even they don't have to sit in one place and wait to be wiped out. There are islands thousands of miles from anywhere— the Hawaiian Islands, for example and Easter Island—where plants seeded themselves and grew long before any humans arrived.
> Earthseed.
> I am Earthseed. Anyone can be. Someday I think there will be a lot of us. And I think we'll have to seed ourselves farther and farther from this dying place. (68–69)

Her religion of Earthseed is centered in this symbol of open motion—traveling in a free but purposeful manner away from a "dying place" to a new space offering new life. In this sense Earthseed is a creative center to her life (she *becomes* Earthseed) in which all of her journeys mix with and enrich each other. Her movements through nature, the self, and God become one in this free but "unifying, purposeful" vision of "life on earth" (234).

The vehicle that empowers her as she takes these psychological and spiritual journeys is art, her writing of her poems and Earthseed journals. Like Charles Johnson and Ishmael Reed, who consider art as a means of constructing an authentic self, Butler sees her writing as a way of consciously shaping and purposefully directing her life. When Lauren is asked by a friend how people can survive in the disintegrating world of twenty-first-century America, she replies, "[U]se your imagination" (52)—that is, refuse to accept the "patterns" imposed by a repressive society and create your own directions. Lauren's writings therefore are critically important in her attempts to fashion a journey for herself that will not only move her beyond "walls" but also enable her to avoid the "abyss" with which her society confronts her.

It is not surprising therefore when she reveals early in the novel, "I have to write to keep from going crazy" (46). Later, when vandals destroy her family and bring her old life to a horrifying close, she senses that her writing is her only chance to avoid madness and move toward a new life:

> I have to write. I don't know what else to do. . . . I'm jittery and crazed. I can't cry. I want to get up and just run and run. . . . Run away from everything. But there isn't any away.
> I have to write. There's nothing familiar left to me but the writing. God is change. I hate God. I have to write. (141)

In a physical world of traps and terror where there seems to be no "away" into which one can escape, writing creates a "way" leading to inward and outward movement that is salvific. First of all, writing becomes a "way" in the sense that it is a means to empower the self by inducing and enriching self-consciousness. Secondly, writing is a "way" in the sense that it can direct movement in a flexible but purposeful manner, thus creating pathways to outer experience that the self freely maps out. Lauren's writings finally achieve both functions, enabling her to imagine a redemptive space called Earthseed and then move consciously toward this space. While the social world that others have constructed has produced violence and anarchy that rob Lauren of anything "familiar," thus making her "crazed and jittery," her writing allows her to picture her life as a clean slate upon which she can write her own identity, freely journeying to spaces within herself to which society has tried to block admission.

Acorn, the Earthseed community that her writings help her to imagine and construct, finally provides her and her fellow travelers with a new life of limitless growth, what Ellison described at the end of *Invisible Man* as a world of "infinite possibilities."[6] The community that they establish is a socially open space whose purpose is to "take root among the stars" (199), to become a world of ongoing growth that is in harmony with the protean nature of the human self and nature. Such a fluid society encourages them "to grow ourselves into something new" (201), thus overcoming the slavery that has characterized their previous lives. Jillian and Allison Gilchrist shed their former roles as prostitutes and become the parents of Justin Rohr, the orphaned boy whom they rename Adam. Bankole, whose marriage was destroyed when druggies killed his wife in order to steal her medicine, marries Lauren, who in turn recovers the kinship relationships she lost when her family was destroyed by a variety of predators. The Douglasses, a racially mixed couple who were persecuted by conventional society, are fully accepted in the new society. Harry and Zahra also marry, transforming their previously empty lives. All of these people, who come from a wide assortment of races and backgrounds, become a multicultural community, an "interesting unit" (193) committed to renewing the human race.

But although this Earthseed community is built on Bankole's land, which is "free and clear" (286) of debt and is also an "empty" and "wild" (281) space offering a fresh start, it is not idealized by Butler as a final resting place, a fixed and stable end point for their travels. Even though the land has an excellent supply of uncontaminated water and has a substantial "garden" (281) for growing fruits and vegetables, it is not perceived either by the characters or the author as a place that can solve their problems permanently. For such a world is not immune to the ravages of the sociopaths and psychopaths who have blighted the society from which they came. When Lauren's group reaches their much sought-for promised land, they discover to their horror that Bankole's house has been burned to the ground, his sister and her family have been butchered, and his farm has become "a huge ruined garden" (216). At best, this place is only "a possible sanctuary" (286), a temporary way station providing them with some degree of rest before they reembark on their journeys to safer spaces.

What these spaces might be is never made exactly clear, just as the end points of journeys taken by picaresque heroes such as Huck Finn, the invisible man, and Ruth Copeland are never precisely defined. Their "new home" (281) cannot be found on any maps because it is a space to be quested after, not a place that can be inhabited. Like the "home" over the River Jordan celebrated by the spirituals, it is a state of mind and a spiritual ideal. The future for Butler's characters, therefore, is liberatingly indeterminate, something that must always be creatively shaped and reshaped as they move and develop.

In essence, *Parable of the Sower* expresses its meanings in terms of two metaphors based upon two important discoveries of modern science: the second law of thermodynamics, which was a major premise of early-twentieth-century science; and the discovery of new space in the solar system, which is an important achievement of late-twentieth-century science. About midway through the novel Lauren, Harry, and Travis, while engaging in a religious conversation, discuss the second law of thermodynamics, which Travis describes as

> The natural flow of heat . . . from something hot to cool . . . so that the universe is cooling down, running down, dissipating its energy. (195)

Such a pessimistic vision of life, which Harry incorrectly links to God, is emphatically denied by the novel. Far from imagining a mechanical universe slowly losing its energy and degenerating either into paralysis or disintegration, what scientists describe as entropy, Butler's novel posits a dynamic, growing universe that is always transforming itself, assuming new forms. Even though the social world described in the novel is clearly entropic because it is built on mechanical "patterns" that have lost their vitality, the novel itself is centered in the firm belief that human beings can reverse this decline by fashioning better worlds that are in harmony with the protean nature of the universe. A small illustration of this occurs at the end of the novel, when Lauren commemorates the death of Bankole's sister by planting trees rather than building a conventional stone grave marker. Declaring that "trees are better than stone—life commemorating life" (293), she celebrates the world as an organic process that is always renewing itself, transforming death into new life. The universe for her is an open journey of limitless possibilities.

Lauren therefore rejects the meaning of the second law and is instead inspired by the hopeful implications of modern space travel. At the beginning of the novel she is saddened by the American government's scuttling of the space program when an American astronaut named Alicea Leal dies while conducting experiments on Mars. Believing that "Space could be our future" (18), she views Alicea as a "model" and begins to embark on her own search for "space," first by initiating an inward journey provided by her Earthseed notebooks and later by heading north in search of a new life. Space travel is not only literally exciting for Lauren but also serves as a bold metaphor of how mankind should pursue its destiny:

> It isn't enough for us to survive, limping along, playing business as usual while things get worse and worse. If that's the shape we give to God, then someday we must become too weak—too poor, too hungry, too sick—to defend ourselves. Then we'll be wiped out.
> There has to be more that we can do, a better destiny that we can shape. Another place. Another way. Something! (67)

Parable of the Sower gives compelling artistic form to the "better destiny" that Lauren exhorts people to "shape." Viewing life affirmatively as a series of interrelated open journeys in free space rather than entropic paralysis, Butler's novel does indeed reveal that man is not a cripple condemned to "limping along" the path to destruction. There is "another way"—actively shaping experience to produce limitless growth. Like most African American picaresque novelists, Butler ultimately envisions the self and the universe as open journeys, thus finding a "way" in a world that only seems to provide "no way."

Conclusion

Recognizing the centrality of the journey motif in African American literature, Lawrence Rodgers has recently observed that "It might be asserted that almost all African-American literature is migration literature." Focusing especially on "real" or "symbolic" journeys from south to north taking place in the twentieth century, Rodgers argues that "the basic drive of migration is the search for a livable home" and that this quest is centered in the desire to achieve "physical and spiritual freedom." Rodgers ultimately concludes that the vast majority of modern African American migration narratives end in frustration and defeat:

> Inevitably . . . idealism fades as the migrant assumes a second-class citizenship in the North that resembles more familiar race, caste, and class exclusion in the South. Just as Douglass soon realized that even in the North he "was still in the enemy's land," achieving the lofty goal of freedom by moving north is far from assured, and, in fact, the conclusion of the majority of migration novels more closely reflects Gillis's final ruin than Douglass's fame and distinction. Migration authors differ markedly from one another in where they locate the cause of the literary migrant's defeat. White racism, intra-racial rivalry, character flaws, immoral and deterministic cityscapes, industrial malice, political divisions, and gender exploitation are some of the reasons for the migrant's downfall.[1]

But, as this study of the open journey in African American fiction has tried to make clear, the literal journeys of failure depicted in many African American migration novels tell only part of the story. Seen in its broadest context, African American picaresque fiction is anything but a literature of "defeat" and "downfall." Although novels like *Invisible Man*, *Native Son*, and *Faith and the Good Thing* may appear to end in failure when considered as teleological journeys from a *place* called the South to a place called the North, when considered as nonteleological journeys in psychological

144

and moral *space,* they reveal remarkably positive meanings. Moreover, novels such as *Their Eyes Were Watching God, Song of Solomon, Dessa Rose,* and *The Parable of the Sower* ultimately portray outward and inward journeys that are strikingly affirmative in a great variety of ways. *The Third Life of Grange Copeland* and *Flight to Canada* are likewise centered in an essentially hopeful vision of life as an open process centered in free will and consciousness, a never-ending journey to self-discovery and self-creation.

The nine novels examined in detail in this study, as well as countless other important African American texts, ranging from the spirituals and slave narratives to the experimental fiction of James Alan McPherson and Randall Kenan, emphatically illustrate how the journey motif in African American literature is fundamentally affirmative in outlook and amazingly protean in form. Characters like Bigger Thomas, Janie Crawford, the invisible man, and their literary descendants in the African American fiction of the last thirty years are remarkable for their ability to make "a way out of no way," that is, creating various kinds of open space for themselves and others and thus triumphing over restrictive social worlds that attempt to put them in their "place." Thus, they overcome the status of victims and become, to varying degrees, genuinely modern heroes.

The large and significant body of fiction studied in this book, therefore, offers a vivid illustration of how African American literature brilliantly "signifies" upon mainstream literature, echoing canonical literature while substantially revising its meanings. In this way, black American literature is centered in a vision of life that is much more affirmative than modern literature in general. As Michael G. Cooke has argued, twentieth-century African American literature has, by and large, rejected the nihilism and detachment that pervade so much modern and postmodern fiction, and sought instead an engagement with the world that is fundamentally affirmative:

> While modernism in white literature took the form of hothouse virtuosity and detachment (if not revulsion) from the human, in Afro-American literature it took the form of a centering upon the possibilities of the human and an emergent sense of intimacy predicated on the human. The crumbling of traditional structures of support in the society at large may have called up wild echoes and startling manifestations in the aesthetic vanguard, but it entailed no more than a mild dislocation for those who had passed generations in a milieu of dispossession. The Afro-American situation that had obliged its people to count on themselves or nothing now became the foundation for building a new structure of experience in

the common ground that stood devoid of any cultural great house. In effect, even as the literature of the ascendant society continued to preoccupy itself with traditional structures in the mode of absence or perversion, Afro-American literature was undertaking to reincarnate and reinvest with value the culture's lost sense of being and belonging.[2]

This distinction can be emphatically made by considering how black American writers have used the picaresque mode to avoid a "hothouse virtuosity" leading to nihilism and instead have made vital new uses of this mode to "reinvest with value the culture's lost sense of being and belonging." The picaresque novel continues to flourish in African American literature while its capacities for affirmation have largely been exhausted in modern European and English journey literature. For example, Ellison's invisible man finds "infinite possibilities"[3] in exploring the always-expanding spaces of his own consciousness but modern European *picaros* such as Céline's Bardamu and Frisch's Stiller find inward and outward journeying equally futile as they reach dead ends in a meaningless universe. Beckett's *The Unnamable* and Lowry's *Under the Volcano* are corrosive parodies of the picaresque novel itself, robbing all movement of significance by reducing their central characters' actions to purposeless drifting in an entropic universe on the verge of disintegrating into a colossal void. But African American picaros continue to journey in a variety of meaningful ways. Although the actual frontier has long since been closed and Americans often complain of being confined to labyrinthine cities, many important black writers continue to provide impressive evidence of what Ellison has called "the magical fluidity and freedom"[4] of American life. Alice Walker's Ruth Grangefield, for example, can still activate a meaningful version of the American dream by escaping from the restrictive places of a segregated society and discovering various forms of liberating space in the larger American world. Rutherford Calhoun, the hero of Charles Johnson's *Middle Passage*, can likewise rejuvenate himself by taking a voyage on the "open, endless sea" away from what he describes as the "living death" on the "landside" world.[5] In a comparable way, Paule Marshall's heroines such as Selina Boyce and Avey Johnson renew themselves with voyages to the Caribbean that expand their consciousness and reinvigorate their lives.

But the modern picaresque fiction written by white American writers consistently reveals massive self-doubt, if not utter exhaustion. John Barth's characters often find themselves at the "end of the road" as they pursue adventures in the external world and eventually become frustrated by the mental journeys they undertake in art, finally sensing that fun houses are more terrifying than life-sustaining. A colossal nihilism seems to hover in the background of Thomas Pynchon's picaresque ramblings. *V* suggests that "this was all there was to dream; all there ever was, the Street," but such a street eventually becomes a "20ᵗʰ Century nightmare" because it provides neither the "safety" of "home"[6] nor the adventure of open journeying leading to rejuvenated spirits and self-creation. Rather, all movement in Pynchon's *V* is reduced to entropy, a slow disintegration of the self and the world. Things get worse when we contemplate a more recent text such as Brett Easton Ellis's *Less than Zero*, a novel that contrasts so sharply with a book like *Invisible Man* because the central character's journey brings him *beyond* invisibility to a point where he is indeed *less* than zero, a negative integer hopelessly paralyzed by self-doubt and nausea.

This study, however, centers on the persistent vitality of the journey motif in African American fiction as it continues to assume new forms that express affirmative values in black experience. While many nonblack writers worry about disappearing as they reach the "end of the road," black writers such as Don L. Lee celebrate their ability to "walk the way of the new world," echoing a powerfully affirmative motif in American literature going back to Crevecoeur's *Letters From an American Farmer*. The open journey, which suffuses African American literature from the earliest slave narratives to the most recent metafictions by Ishmael Reed and Charles Johnson, continues to be an important narrative device that can express in a compelling way what Cooke described as the "possibilities of the human" in African American experience. Such open narratives, which simultaneously evoke allusions to the journey across the River Jordan celebrated by the spirituals, the odyssey down the road extolled by the blues, and the quest for open space celebrated in classic American and African American literature, help to make contemporary black fiction a remarkably vital and resonant body of literature.

Notes

INTRODUCTION

1. Tennessee Williams, *The Glass Menagerie* (New York: New Directions, 1945), 115.

2. John Steinbeck, *Travels with Charley: In Search of America* (New York: Bantam Books, 1971), 10.

3. Ralph Ellison, *Shadow and Act* (New York: New American Library, 1966), 113.

4. Samuel Charters, *The Poetry of the Blues* (New York: Oak Publications, 1963), 71. Hazel Carby has recently argued that black women blues singers gave special meaning to blues movement. Often the victims of male desertion, they were essentially ambivalent about the open journey so often celebrated in blues sung by males. Some songs such as Bessie Smith's "House Blues" expressed "rage against male infidelity and desertion" (236) which resulted in women being trapped in domestic space. Other blues songs sung by black women, however, expressed a deep desire for female independence that could be achieved by leaving settled space and simply taking off down an open road. Ethel Waters's "No Man's Mamma Now," for example, boldly proclaims "I can come when I please, I can go where I please / I can flit, fly and flutter like the birds in the trees / Because I'm no man's mamma now" ("It Just Be's Dat Way Sometime: The Sexual Politics of Women's Blues," in *Gender and Discourse: The Power of Talk,* ed. Alexandra Dumas Todd and Sue Fisher [Norwood N.J.: Ablex, 1988], 227–42).

5. Ellison, *Shadow and Act,* 78.

6. Blyden Jackson, "The Negro's Image of the Universe as Reflected in His Fiction," *CLA Journal* 4 (fall 1960): 29.

7. Roger Rosenblatt, *Black Fiction* (Cambridge: Harvard University Press, 1974), 19, 199.

8. Phyllis Rauch Klotman, *Another Man Gone: The Black Runner in Contemporary Afro-American Literature* (Port Washington, N.Y.: Kennikat Press, 1977), 21.

9. Robert Bone, *Down Home: A History of Afro-American Short Fiction from its Beginnings to the End of the Harlem Renaissance* (New York: Putnam, 1975), 120–21.

10. Lawrence R. Rodgers, "Dorothy West's *The Living is Easy* and the Ideal of Southern Folk Community," *African American Review* 26 (spring 1992): 168. See also Professor Rodgers's "Paul Laurence Dunbar's *The Sport of the Gods* and the Doubly Conscious World of Plantation Fiction," *American Literary Realism* 24 (spring 1992): 42–57 and his recent book *Canaan Bound: The African American Great Migration Novel* (Urbana and Chicago: University of Illinois Press), 1997.

11. Richard Wright, *The Long Dream* (Garden City, N.Y.: Doubleday, 1958), 378.

12. Ralph Ellison, *Invisible Man* (New York: Random House, 1952), 435.

13. Eldridge Cleaver, "The Flashlight," in *The City in American Literature*, ed. James Pickering (New York: Harper and Row, 1977): 269.

14. Houston A. Baker Jr., *Blues, Ideology, and Afro-American Literature: A Vernacular Theory* (Chicago: University of Chicago Press, 1984), 3–4, 7.

15. Henry Louis Gates Jr., *The Signifying Monkey: A Theory of African-American Literary Criticism* (New York: Oxford University Press, 1989), xxiii.

16. Anthony Appiah, "Strictures on Structures: The Prospects for a Structuralist Poetics of African Fiction," in *Black Literature and Literary Theory*, ed. Henry Louis Gates Jr. (New York: Methuen, 1984), 146.

17. Gates, *Signifying Monkey*, xxii.

18. William Andrews, *To Tell A Free Story: The First Century of Afro-American Autobiography, 1760–1865* (Urbana and Chicago: University of Illinois Press, 1986), 29.

19. Ellison, *Invisible Man*, 122.

20. Ellison, *Shadow and Act*, 174.

21. Frederick Douglass, *Narrative of the Life of Frederick Douglass*, ed. Houston A. Baker Jr. (New York: Penguin Books, 1982), 151, 143.

22. James Weldon Johnson, *Along This Way* (New York: Viking Press, 1961), 152.

23. William Craft and Ellen Craft, *Running a Thousand Miles for Freedom*, in *Great Slave Narratives*, ed. Arna Bontemps (Boston: Beacon Press, 1969), 135.

24. Quoted in *The Life of Langston Hughes*, vol. 1: *1902–1941*, ed. Arnold Rampersad (New York: Oxford University Press, 1986), 50.

25. Harriet Jacobs, *Incidents in the Life of a Slave Girl*, in *The Classic Slave Narratives*, ed. Henry Louis Gates Jr. (New York: New American Library, 1987), 513, 516.

26. Melvin Dixon, *Ride Out the Wilderness: Geography and Identity in Afro-American Literature* (Urbana and Chicago: University of Illinois Press, 1987), 2, 3, 3, 2.

27. Farah Jasmine Griffin, *"Who Set You Flowin'?": The African-American Migration Narrative* (New York: Oxford University Press, 1995), 100, 107, 100, 107, 142, 111, 142, 147.

28. James Baldwin, *Nobody Knows My Name: More Notes of a Native Son* (New York: Dell Books, 1961), 12.

29. Quoted in Jervis Anderson, "The Public Intellectual," *New Yorker,* 17 January 1994, 48. In *Race Matters* (New York: Random House, 1994) West again describes the "cultural hybrid character of black life" as a special strength, noting that black experience is a dynamic ferment of many elements rather than a single static mode of being grounded in a particular place with fixed traditions. Comparing African American life to jazz, he argues that both represent "a mode of being in the world, an improvisational mode of protean, fluid, and flexible dispositions toward reality" that refuse to be arrested or limited by dogmatic pronouncements or supremacist ideologies (150). Like Ralph Ellison, a writer West deeply admires, he perceives black identity as an ongoing process, not a fixed condition rooted in changeless absolutes.

30. Ellison, *Shadow and Act*, 113.

31. Paul Gilroy, *The Black Atlantic: Modernity and Double Consciousness* (Cambridge: Harvard University Press, 1993), 122, 133, xi.

32. Richard Wright, *Native Son* (Harper and Row, 1966), 107, 226.

33. Ellison, *Invisible Man*, 5, 429, 428.

34. Charles Johnson, *Faith and The Good Thing* (New York: Atheneum, 1987), 188.

35. Robert Stepto, *From Beyond the Veil: A Study of Afro-American Narrative* (Urbana: University of Illinois Press, 1979), 167.

CHAPTER 1. STUNTED PICARESQUES

1. In their autobiographical writings, both Hurston and Wright described their lives as fully open journeys that transcended the factors that produced stunted picaresque narratives in novels such as *Their Eyes Were Watching God* and *Native Son.* As the title of *Dust Tracks on a Road* suggests, Hurston imagined her life as indeterminate movement in free space, *a* road leading to indefinite possibilities rather than *the* road pointing toward a particular place containing a fixed meaning. (See Zora Neale Hurston, *Dust Tracks on a Road: An Autobiography*, ed. Robert Hemenway [Urbana and Chicago: University of Illinois Press, 1984]. All subsequent references to the text are to this edition and page numbers are cited parenthetically after the quote.) She emphatically rejects the attempts of several people to place her in what she calls "the pigeonhole way of life" (33), which would reduce her to a static existence as a "statue" (34). A quester for a fluid world of open possibility, she instinctively shrinks from a world where "everything is known and settled" (226) and instead commits herself to a "pilgrimage" on a "strange road" (60) to uncharted experience, the "end of the horizon" (36). Like most Afro-American and American picaresque figures, she regards her life as a process of endless becoming: "The stuff of my being is matter, ever changing, every moving, never lost" (279). At the conclusion of *Dust Tracks* she defines her personality as protean, the product of forces that are always in motion: "My real home is in the water . . . the earth is only my stepmother. My old man, the sun, sired me out of the sea" (347).

Black Boy, likewise, envisions Wright's life as a quest for constant motion in open space, a quest that rejects all forms of experience that would "place" him in a rigidly segregated society by assigning him static roles and a fixed identity. In leaving the South for the North, Wright moved toward what Robert Stepto has called a "symbolic space" (*From Behind the Veil* [Urbana and Chicago: University of Illinois Press, 1979], 152), an open world of possibility. Although most critics have argued that Wright's alienation from a stable social world was finally traumatic for him and led him to envision life in essentially negative terms, the fact is that he welcomed open motion as an alternative to placement in a restrictive society and saw his own life in affirmative terms as an open-ended picaresque narrative. As he observed in *White Man, Listen!*,

> I'm a rootless man but I'm neither psychologically distraught nor in any ways particularly perturbed because of it. Personally, I do not hanker after, and seem not to need, as many emotional attachments, sustaining roots, or idealistic allegiances as most people. . . . I can make a home almost anywhere on this earth. (*White Man, Listen!* [Garden City, N.Y.: Doubleday, 1957], 17)

For a full discussion of the open journey in *Black Boy*, see my "The Quest for Pure Motion in Richard Wright's *Black Boy*," *MELUS* 10, no. 3 (fall 1983): 5–17.

2. Zora Neale Hurston, *Their Eyes Were Watching God* (Greenwich, Conn.: Fawcett, 1965), 5. All subsequent references to the text are to this edition and page numbers are cited parenthetically after the quote.

3. Richard Wright, *Native Son* (New York: Harper and Row, 1966), 18–19. All sub-

sequent references to the text are to this edition and page numbers are cited parenthetically after the quote.

4. Blyden Jackson, "The Negro's Image of His Universe as Reflected in His Fiction," *CLA Journal* 4 (September 1960): 41.

5. Phyllis Rauch Klotman, *Another Man Gone: The Black Runner in Contemporary Afro-American Literature* (Port Washington, N.Y.: Kennikat Press, 1977), 58, 57.

CHAPTER 2. RALPH ELLISON'S *INVISIBLE MAN*

1. Richard Wright, *Black Boy: A Record of Childhood and Youth* (New York: Harper and Row, 1966), 43.

2. Ibid., 42.

3. We are told at the end of the Battle Royal that the town where the episode takes places is called "Greenwood." But this may not be a place where the hero has lived for very long. Then too, the name Ellison gives the town certainly does not pin it down to as definite location. Many states in the Deep South have a town named Greenwood.

4. Ralph Ellison, *Invisible Man*. (New York: Random House, 1952), 121. All subsequent references to the text are to this Modern Library edition. Page numbers appear parenthetically after the quote.

5. In *Going to the Territory* (New York: Random House, 1986) Ellison has elaborated in some detail on the crucial impact that New York City had on his own personal development. Coming to New York in the summer of 1936 to earn enough money to complete his senior year at Tuskegee Institute, he soon became aware of the "cultural possibilities" and "social freedom" that the city offered him. Like the hero of the novel, he eventually came to see the city in existential terms as a "rite of initiation" for which he had to be his "own guide and instructor."

New York became for him a "journey without a map" leading to self-discovery and self-creation. Now freed from the "claustrophobic provincialism" of the South that inhibited his growth by imposing narrow roles on him, he begins existentially to develop "a second self" through a process of "masking" that he defines as "playing upon possibility, a strategy through which the individual projects a self-elected identity and make[s] of himself a work of art." Like the hero of the novel, he sees the city as a liberating new space that allows him to define himself in existential, protean terms.

6. Most Alger novels espouse a clearly defined formula for success, providing a "paradigm" that books like Washington's *Up from Slavery* use for serious purposes, but *Invisible Man* inverts for ironic effects. Alger's *Ragged Dick,* for example, centers on the hero's "plan" to achieve "a new life" by working hard and then impressing wealthy men who will provide a place for the hero in middle-class life. Sponsors such as Mr. Greyson and Mr. Rockwell complete the hero's identity by providing him with a new name (Richard Hunter, Esq.), a steady job, and the prospects of a continued "rise" in American life. Ellison's invisible man earnestly pursues his formula for success for most of the novel but abandons it because he realizes that such "success" will destroy his identity by turning him into a robot. He therefore separates from sponsors such as Norton, Bledsoe, and Jack, simultaneously rejecting the material rewards they have promised him. He also stubbornly refuses the names that others have imposed upon him, preferring to have no name. Namelessness represents the fluid, indeterminate identity he achieves by existentially descending into the self.

7. Irving Howe, "A Negro in America," *Nation,* 10 May 1952, 454.

8. Marcus Klein, *After Alienation* (Cleveland: World, 1964), 109.

9. Edward Margolies, *Native Sons: A Critical Study of Twentieth-Century American-Negro Authors* (Philadelphia: Lippincott, 1968), 148.

10. Floyd Horowitz, "Ralph Ellison's Modern Invisible Man," *Midcontinent American Studies Journal* 4 (1963): 221.

11. Roger Rosenblatt, *Black Fiction* (Cambridge: Harvard University Press, 1974), 185.

12. Charles Johnson, *Being and Race: Black Writing Since 1970* (Bloomington: Indiana University Press, 1990), 16–17.

13. Robert Frost, *The Poetry of Robert Frost*, ed. Edward Latham (New York: Holt, 1964), 282.

14. Leslie Fiedler, *Waiting for the End* (Boston: Beacon Press, 1964), 137.

15. Ellison, *Shadow and Act*, 137.

16. In *Shadow and Act* he describes his life in Oklahoma as noticeably freer than it could have been in the South in those times; it was a place with no tradition of slavery. Being a "border state," it was a good place for Ellison to assimilate the values often associated with frontier life—independence, mobility, and "a boy's dream of possibility" (25–26).

17. Ibid., 25.

18. George Rogers Taylor, ed., *The Turner Thesis Concerning the Role of the Frontier in American History* (Lexington, Mass.: Heath, 1974), 4.

19. Ellison, *Shadow and Act*, 94.

20. Marjorie Pryse, "Ralph Ellison's Heroic Fugitive," *American Literature* 46 (spring 1973): 13.

21. Ellison, *Shadow and Act*, 113.

22. Stephen Whicher, ed., *Selections from Ralph Waldo Emerson* (Boston: Houghton Mifflin, 1960), 169–70.

23. Ibid., 170.

24. Johnson, *Being and Race*, 15.

25. Keith Byerman, *Fingering the Jagged Grain: Tradition and Form in Recent Black Fiction*. (Athens: University of Georgia Press, 1985), 9, 7.

CHAPTER 3. ALICE WALKER'S *THE THIRD LIFE* OF *GRANGE COPELAND*

1. Harriet Wilson, *Our Nig; or, Sketches from the Life of a Free Black* (New York: Random House, 1983), 129, 120, 130.

2. Nella Larsen, *Quicksand and Passing* (New Brunswick, N.J.: Rutgers University Press, 1986), 118, 123, 133, 134.

3. Jesse Fauset, *Plum Bun* (London and Boston: Pandora Press, 1985), 361. All subsequent references to the text are to this edition, and page numbers are cited parenthetically after the quotes. Cheryl Wall's recent study, *Women of the Harlem Renaissance* (Bloomington and Indianapolis: Indiana University Press, 1995), argues cogently that women writers of the Harlem Renaissance depicted failed journeys ending in "stasis and claustrophobia" (4). Male writers of the time, like Claude McKay and Langston Hughes, wrote strikingly different fiction centered in constant movement.

4. Robert Stepto, *From Behind the Veil: A Study in Afro-American Narrative* (Urbana and Chicago: University of Illinois Press, 1979), 167.

5. Frances E. W. Harper, *Iola Leroy, or Shadows Uplifted* (New York: Oxford University Press, 1988), 279, 247, 274, 280, 138, 280.

6. Alice Walker, *In Search of Our Mothers' Gardens* (New York: Harcourt Brace Jovanovich, 1983), 5. All subsequent references to the text are to this edition and page numbers are cited parenthetically after the quotes.

7. Alice Walker, *Meridian* (New York: Pocket Books, 1977), 108–9.

8. Alice Walker, *In Love and Trouble* (New York: Harcourt Brace Jovanovich, 1973), 6. All subsequent references to the text are to this edition and page numbers are cited parenthetically after the quotes.

9. Alice Walker, *You Can't Keep a Good Woman Down* (New York: Harcourt Brace Jovanovich, 1981), 39. All subsequent references to the text are to this edition and page numbers are cited parenthetically after the quotes.

10. Alice Walker, *The Third Life of Grange Copeland* (New York: Harcourt Brace Jovanovich, 1970), 17–18. All subsequent references to the text are to this edition and page numbers are cited parenthetically after the quote.

11. In an essay entitled "The Civil Rights Movement: What Good Was It?" and later collected in *In Search of Our Mothers' Gardens*, Walker speaks of her own involvement with the movement as a pivotal moment in her life, a conversion experience that enabled her to be "born again, literally" (125). Like Ruth, she first became aware of the movement by watching newscasts of Dr. King and his workers on marches and demonstrations. Her subsequent involvement with the movement empowered her to overcome a condition of paralysis, "the pattern of black servitude in this country" (128), and deepened her consciousness to a point where she was pushed "out into the world, into college, into places, into people" (125). It freed her, allowing her "to be involved, to move about, to see the world with [her] own eyes" (126).

12. Walker's ambivalence toward the South is vividly dramatized throughout *In Search of Our Mothers' Gardens*. At times she warmly celebrates southern land and community and is "intrigued by the thought of what continuity of place could mean to the consciousness of the emerging writer" (163–64). But she also feels "hemmed in" by memories of the southern past that continue to "plague" (166) her. Her seven years in Mississippi, which epitomizes the South for her, reduce her to a state that she describes as "suicidal," and she leaves, resolving "never to set foot in Mississippi again" (224). Furthermore, she is disturbed by the growing homogenization of life in the South, claiming that "the pervasive football culture bores me and the proliferating Kentucky Fried Chicken stands appall me" (170). Her reading of southern literature also underscores her deep suspicion of southern place. She expresses a real distaste for Faulkner's fiction, claiming that it is deeply flawed by Faulkner's outlook as a white southerner. The southern writer she most admires is Flannery O'Connor, whose Catholicism allowed her to keep a healthy critical distance from the South: "Miss O'Connor was not so much of Georgia, as in it" (20). Zora Neale Hurston, the black writer Walker most admires, returned to the South late in life only to die of malnutrition and be buried in an unmarked grave. Although the romantic side of Walker's temperament longs for a pastoral southern world, a "garden" cultivated by people like her mother, her realistic impulses warn her that she will have to create her own "garden" in the space she creates for herself in her own life's journey.

13. Alice Walker, *The Color Purple* (New York: Washington Square Press, 1982), 250.

14. Trudier Harris, "On *The Color Purple*, Stereotypes, and Silence," *Black American Literature Forum* 18 (fall 1984): 160.

15. Ibid., 161.

CHAPTER 4. TONI MORRISON'S *SONG OF SOLOMON*

1. Toni Morrison, *Tarbaby* (New York: New American Library, 1977), 166. All subsequent references to the text are to this edition and page numbers are cited parenthetically after the quote.
2. Toni Morrison, *Sula* (New York: New American Library, 1973), 165, 108.
3. Toni Morrison, *Beloved* (New York: Plume Books, 1987), 183, 123, 66.
4. Toni Morrison, *Jazz* (New York: Alfred Knopf, 1992), 174.
5. Toni Morrison, *Song of Solomon* (New York: New American Library, 1977), 163. All subsequent references to the text are to this edition and page numbers are cited parenthetically after the quote.
6. Dorothy Lee, "*Song of Solomon:* To Ride the Air," *Black American Literature Forum* 16, no. 2 (fall 1980): 70.
7. Joyce Wegs, "Toni Morrison's *Song of Solomon:* A Blues Song," *Essays in Literature* 9, no. 2 (fall 1982): 219.
8. Leslie Harris, "Myth as Structure in *Song of Solomon,*" *MELUS* 7, no. 3 (fall 1980): 74.
9. Susan Blake, "Folklore and the Community in *Song of Solomon,*" *MELUS* 7, no. 3 (fall 1980): 79.
10. Harris, "Myth as Structure," 71.
11. Mel Watkins, "A Talk with Toni Morrison," *New York Times Book Review,* September 1977, 50.

CHAPTER 5. CHARLES JOHNSON'S *FAITH AND THE GOOD THING*

1. Charles Johnson, *Faith and the Good Thing* (New York: Atheneum, 1974), 3. All subsequent references to the text are to this edition and page numbers are cited parenthetically after the quote.
2. Joseph Campbell, *The Hero with a Thousand Faces* (Princeton: Princeton University Press, 1949), 49, 35, 17.
3. Walt Whitman, *Leaves of Grass: The First (1855) Edition* (New York: Viking Press, 1959), 79.
4. Ralph Ellison, *Invisible Man* (New York: Random House, 1952), 435.
5. Samuel Clemens, *Adventures of Huckleberry Finn* (New York: New American Library, 1959), 283.
6. Charles Johnson, *Being and Race* (Bloomington and Indianapolis: Indiana University Press, 1990), 11, 121, 53, 40, 49.
7. Charles Johnson, *Oxherding Tales* (Bloomington and Indianapolis: Indiana University Press, 1982), 109, 17, 144.
8. Charles Johnson, *Middle Passage* (New York: Plume Books, 1991), 1, 187, 124, 98, 207.

CHAPTER 6. ISHMAEL REED'S *FLIGHT TO CANADA*

1. James Alan McPherson, *Elbow Room* (New York: Fawcett Crest, 1979), 285.
2. Charles Johnson, *Oxherding Tales* (Bloomington: Indiana University Press, 1982), 109.

3. Ishmael Reed, *Mumbo Jumbo* (New York: Atheneum, 1972), 155, 25, 204, 139, 6, 4, 204.

4. Hazel Carby, "Ideologies of Black Folk: The Historical Novel of Slavery," in *Slavery and the Literary Imagination*, ed. Deborah E. McDowell and Arnold Rampersad (Baltimore: Johns Hopkins University Press, 1989), 125–26.

5. Ishmael Reed, *Flight to Canada* (New York: Atheneum, 1989), 144. All subsequent references to the text are to this edition and page numbers appear parenthetically after the quote.

6. Kimberly Benston, "I Yam What I Yam: The Topos of Un(naming) in Afro-American Literature." *Black American Literature Forum* 16 (spring 1982): 3.

7. Samuel Beckett, *Three Novels by Samuel Beckett: Molloy, Malone Dies, The Unnamable* (New York: Grove Press, 1965), 314.

8. McPherson, *Elbow Room,* 378.

CHAPTER 7. SHERLEY ANNE WILLIAMS'S *DESSA ROSE*

1. Arnold Rampersad, "Slavery and the Literary Imagination: The Souls of Black Folk," in *Slavery and the Literary Imagination*, ed. Deborah McDowell and Arnold Rampersad (Baltimore: Johns Hopkins University Press, 1989), 13.

2. Henry Louis Gates Jr., *Figures in Black: Words, Signs, and the Racial Self* (New York: Oxford University Press, 1987), 49.

3. Henry Louis Gates Jr., *The Signifying Monkey: A Theory of African-American Literary Criticism* (New York: Oxford University Press, 1989), xvii.

4. Sherley Anne Williams, *Dessa Rose* (New York: Berkley Books, 1987), ix–x, ix, x. All subsequent references to the text are to this edition and page numbers are cited parenthetically after the quote.

5. William Styron, *The Confessions of Nat Turner* (New York: New American Library, 1967), 379, 374, 377.

6. Frederick Douglass, *Narrative of the Life of Frederick Douglass*, ed. Houston A. Baker Jr. (New York: Penguin Books, 1982), 107.

7. William Wells Brown, *The Travels of William Wells Brown*, ed. Paul Jefferson (New York: Markus Weiner, 1991), 46.

8. William Craft and Ellen Craft, *Running a Thousand Miles for Freedom,* in *Great Slave Narratives*, ed. Arna Bontemps (Boston: Beacon Press, 1969), 271, 304, 310, 247, 279, 287, 220.

9. Samuel Clemens, *Adventures of Huckleberry Finn* (New York: Signet Books, 1959), 208–9.

10. Judith Fetterly, "Disenchantment: Tom Sawyer in *Huckleberry Finn*," *PMLA* 87 (January 1972): 70, 72.

11. Leo Marx, "Mr. Eliot, Mr. Trilling, and Huckleberry Finn," *American Scholar* 20 (autumn 1953): 430.

12. Gates, *Figures*, 100–101.

13. Elizabeth Ammons, "Stowe's Dream of the Mother-Savior: *Uncle Tom's Cabin* and American Women Writers Before the 1920's," in *New Essays on Uncle Tom's Cabin*, ed. Eric J. Sundquist (Cambridge: Cambridge University Press, 1986), 156–57.

14. Sandra M. Gilbert and Susan Gubar, *The Madwoman in the Attic: The Woman Writer and the Nineteenth-Century Imagination* (New Haven: Yale University Press, 1979), 67, 67–68, 83, 54.

15. Gates, *Signifying Monkey*, xii.

CHAPTER 8. TWENTY-FIRST-CENTURY JOURNEYS IN OCTAVIA E. BUTLER'S *PARABLE OF THE SOWER*

1. Octavia E. Butler, *Patternmaster* (New York: Warner Books, 1976), 46, 67, 198.

2. Octavia E. Butler, *Wild Seed* (New York: Warner Books, 1980), 14, 247, 130.

3. Octavia E. Butler, *Imago* (New York: Warner Books, 1989), 11.

4. Quoted in Sandra Govan, "Connection, Links, and Extended Networks: Patterns in Octavia Butler's Science Fiction," *Black American Literature Forum* 18 (summer 1984): 87.

5. Octavia E. Butler, *The Parable of the Sower* (New York: Warner Books, 1993), 8. All subsequent references to the text are to this edition and page numbers are cited parenthetically after the quote.

6. Ralph Ellison, *Invisible Man* (New York: Random House, 1952), 435.

CONCLUSION

1. Lawrence R. Rodgers, *Canaan Bound: The African-American Great Migration Novel* (Urbana and Chicago: University of Illinois Press, 1997), 3, 4, 31.

2. Michael G. Cooke, *Afro-American Literature in the Twentieth Century: The Achievement of Intimacy* (New Haven: Yale University Press, 1984), 5.

3. Ralph Ellison, *Invisible Man* (New York: Random House, 1952), 435.

4. Ralph Ellison, *Shadow and Act* (New York: New American Library, 1966), 113.

5. Charles Johnson, *Middle Passage* (New York: Plume Books, 1990), 1, 4.

6. Thomas Pynchon, *V* (New York: Bantam Books, 1964), 31, 303.

Selected Bibliography

Anderson, Jervis. "The Public Intellectual." *The New Yorker,* 17 January 1994, 39–48.

Andrews, William. *To Tell a Free Story: The First Century of Afro-American Autobiography.* Urbana and Chicago: University of Illinois Press, 1986.

Baker, Houston. *Blues, Ideology, and Afro-American Literature: A Vernacular Theory.* Chicago: University of Chicago Press, 1984.

———. *The Journey Back: Issues in Black Literature and Criticism.* Chicago: University of Chicago Press, 1980.

———. *Singers at Daybreak: Studies in Black American Literature.* Washington, D.C.: Howard University Press, 1983.

Baldwin, James. *Nobody Knows My Name: More Notes of a Native Son.* New York: Dell, 1961.

———. *Notes of a Native Son.* Boston: Beacon Press, 1955.

Bell, Bernard. *The Afro-American Novel and Its Tradition.* Amherst: University of Massachusetts Press, 1987.

Beyerman, Keith. *Fingering the Jagged Grain: Tradition and Form in Recent Black Fiction.* Athens: University of Georgia Press, 1985.

Bone, Robert. *Down Home: A History of Afro-American Short Fiction from its Beginnings to the End of the Harlem Renaissance.* New York: Putnam, 1975.

Bontemps, Arna. *Anyplace but Here.* New York: Hill and Wang, 1966.

———. *They Seek a City.* New York: Doubleday, 1945.

Boorstin, Daniel J. *The Discoverers: A History of Man's Search to Know Himself and His World.* New York: Vintage Books, 1983.

Bottomley, Gillian. *From Another Place: Migration and the Politics of Culture.* Cambridge: Cambridge University Press, 1992.

Butler, Robert. "Making a Way Out of No Way: The Open Journey in Alice Walker's *The Third Life of Grange Copeland.*" *Black American Literature Forum* 22 (spring 1988): 65–81.

———. "The Quest for Pure Motion in Richard Wright's *Black Boy.*" *MELUS* 10 (fall 1983): 5–17.

Callahan, John. *In the African-American Grain: The Pursuit of Voice in Twentieth-Century Black Fiction.* Urbana and Chicago: University of Illinois Press, 1988.

Campbell, Daniel, and Rex Johnson. *Black Migration in America: A Social Demographic History*. Durham, N.C.: Duke University Press, 1981.

Campbell, Joseph. *The Hero with a Thousand Faces*. Princeton: Princeton University Press, 1949.

Carby, Hazel. "It Jus Be's Dat Way Sometime: Sexual Politics of Women's Blues." In *Gender and Discourse: The Power of Talk*, edited by Alexandra Dundas Todd and Sue Fisher. Norwood, N.J.: Ablex, 1988.

————. *Reconstructing Womanhood: The Emergence of the Black Woman Novelist*. New York: Oxford University Press, 1987.

Charters, Samuel. *The Poetry of the Blues*. New York: Oak Publications, 1963.

Cooke, Michael G. *Afro-American Literature in the Twentieth Century: The Achievement of Intimacy*. New Haven: Yale University Press, 1984.

Craft, William, and Ellen Craft. *Running a Thousand Miles for Freedom*. In *Great Slave Narratives*, edited by Arna Bontemps. Boston: Beacon Press, 1969.

Davis, Charles T., and Henry Louis Gates Jr., eds. *The Slave's Narrative*. New York: Oxford University Press, 1985.

Davis, Percy G. *Travel Literature and the Evolution of the Novel*. Lexington: University Press of Kentucky, 1983.

Dixon, Melvin. *Ride Out the Wilderness: Geography and Identity in Afro-American Literature*. Urbana and Chicago: University of Illinois Press, 1987.

Douglass, Frederick. *Narrative of the Life of Frederick Douglass*. Edited by Houston Baker. New York: Penguin Books, 1982.

Ellison, Ralph. *Going to the Territory*. New York: Random House, 1986.

————. *Shadow and Act*. New York: New American Library, 1966.

Fabre, Michel. *The Unfinished Quest of Richard Wright*. New York: William Morrow, 1973.

Gates, Henry Louis, Jr. *Black Literature and Literary Theory*. London and New York: Methuen, 1984.

————. *Figures in Black: Words, Signs, and the Racial Self*. New York: Oxford University Press, 1987.

————. *The Signifying Monkey: A Theory of African-American Literary Criticism*. New York: Oxford University Press, 1989.

Gilbert, Sandra, and Susan Gubar. *The Madwoman in the Attic: The Woman Writer and the Nineteenth-Century Imagination*. New Haven: Yale University Press, 1979.

Gilroy, Paul. *The Black Atlantic: Modernity and Double Consciousness*. Cambridge: Harvard University Press, 1993.

Griffin, Farah Jasmine. *"Who Set You Flowin'?": The African-American Migration Narrative*. New York: Oxford University Press, 1993.

Jackson, Blyden. "The Negro's Image of the Universe as Reflected in His Fiction." *College Language Association Journal* 4 (1960): 28–42.

Jacobs, Harriet. *Incidents in the Life of a Slave Girl*. In *The Classic Slave Narratives*, edited by Henry Louis Gates Jr. New York: New American Library, 1987.

Jaye, Michael, and Ann Chambers Watts, eds. *Literature and the Urban Experience*. New Brunswick, N.J.: Rutgers University Press, 1981.

Johnson, Charles. *Being and Race: Black Writing since 1970.* Bloomington and Indianapolis: Indiana University Press, 1990.

Johnson, James Weldon. *Along This Way.* New York: Viking, 1961.

Klotman, Phyllis Rauch. *Another Man Gone: The Black Runner in Afro-American Literature.* Port Washington, N.Y.: Kennikat Press, 1977.

Lehmann, Nicholas. *The Promised Land: The Great Black Migration and How It Changed America.* New York: Alfred A. Knopf, 1991.

Lenz, Gunter. "Symbolic Space, Communal Rituals and the Surreality of the Urban Ghetto: Harlem in Black Literature from the 1920s to the 1960s." *Callaloo* 2 (spring 1988): 309–45.

Locke, Alain, ed. *The New Negro: An Interpretation.* New York: Atheneum, 1925.

Marks, Carole. *Farewell—We're Good and Gone: The Great Black Migration.* Bloomington and Indianapolis: Indiana University Press, 1989.

McDowell, Deborah, and Arnold Rampersad, eds. *Slavery and the Literary Imagination.* Baltimore: Johns Hopkins University Press, 1989.

Morrison, Toni. *Playing in the Dark: Whiteness and the Literary Imagination.* Cambridge: Harvard University Press, 1992.

Pryse, Marjorie, and Hortense Spillers, eds. *Conjuring: Black Women, Fiction, and Literary Tradition.* Bloomington: Indiana University Press, 1985.

Pryse, Marjorie. "Ralph Ellison's Heroic Fugitive." *American Literature* 46 (1973): 2–24

Rampersad, Arnold. *The Life of Langston Hughes.* Vol. 1. New York: Oxford University Press, 1986.

Rodgers, Lawrence R. "Dorothy West's *The Living is Easy* and the Ideal of Southern Folk Community." *African American Review* 26 (spring 1992): 161–72.

———. *Canaan Bound: The African-American Great Migration Novel.* Urbana and Chicago: University of Illinois Press, 1997.

———. "Paul Laurence Dunbar's *The Sport of the Gods:* The Doubly Conscious World of Plantation Fiction; Migration and Ascent." *American Literary Realism* 24 (spring 1992): 42–57.

Rosenblatt, Roger. *Black Fiction.* Cambridge: Harvard University Press, 1974.

Scruggs, Charles. *Sweet Home: Invisible Cities in the Afro-American Novel.* Baltimore: Johns Hopkins University Press, 1993.

Sennett, Richard. *The Fall of Public Man.* New York: Alfred A. Knopf, 1974.

Sollors, Werner. *Beyond Ethnicity: Consent and Descent in American Culture.* New York: Oxford University Press, 1986.

Spengemann, William C. *The Adventurous Muse: The Poetics of American Fiction, 1789–1900.* New Haven: Yale University Press, 1977.

Steinbeck, John. *Travels with Charley: In Search of America.* New York: Bantam Books, 1971.

Stepto, Robert. *From Beyond the Veil: A Study of Afro-American Narrative.* Urbana: University of Illinois Press, 1979.

Wall, Cheryl. *Women of the Harlem Renaissance.* Bloomington and Indiana: Indiana University Press, 1995.

Watkins, Mel. "A Talk with Toni Morrison." *New York Times Book Review,* September 1977, 50–53.

West, Cornel. *Race Matters.* New York: Vintage Books, 1994.

Index

161